Hopiness
et Glory

Dr. KADIEBY. E.

TO OVERCOME THE WEIGHT OF THE PAST THAT PURSUES YOU AND THAT CRUCHES YOU

Dr. Eddy KADIEBU KANDOLO

TO OVERCOME

THE WEIGHT OF THE PAST THAT PURSUES YOU AND THAT CRUSHES YOU

EDITIONS LES BENIS DE L'ETERNEL

TO OVERCOME THE WEIGHT OF THE PAST THAT PURSUES YOU AND THAT CRUCHES YOU

Original : « **Vaincre Le Poids Du Passé Qui Vous Poursuit Et Vous Ecrase** »

by Dr Eddy Kadiebu Kandolo
© Editions Les Bénis de l'Eternel, 2017
Centre Chrétien Bérée
5, Allée Louis Daubenton 87280 Limoges-France
ISBN 978-2-9556619-0-1

All rights reserved. No part of this publication may be reproduced, stored in a retrieval system, or transmitted in any form or by any means – electronic, mechanical, photocopy, photograph, recording or any other – without the prior permission of the author or of his beneficiaries or legal successors, as this would constitute a counterfeiting punished by the articles L.335-2 and the following from the code of the intellectual property, according to French law.

FOREWORD

Whoever is still married to his negative past will not enjoy a glorious future with God. To allow the negative past to invade one's life will handicap his efforts in the present and will compromise his future. In this manual, Apostle Eddy Kadiebu, graduated in human & social sciences, and doctor in theology, explains clearly this reality and suggests divine solutions in order to step out from all spiritual, psychological and moral prisons in which many are still stuck today. Mare those who drag their past along like a burden, waste their present with vain things and plan their future with weird and unreal dreams. Let us allow the Holy Spirit to teach us through this manual so that every season of your life be a blessing of God.

All biblical Scriptures in this book are extracted from the New King James version.

TO OVERCOME THE WEIGHT OF THE PAST THAT PURSUES YOU AND THAT CRUCHES YOU

bring to light as to how we can see God as He is and believe that He is working behind the scenes from childhood to our adulthood.

Prof. Dr. Chandrakumar Manickam

Vice-Président International - International Graduate School of Ministry (U.S.A.)

My relationship with Apostle Eddy Kadiebu has started a few years ago and as time went by, I learned to know and to appreciate this man of God, his wife, his family, as well as the flock on which God has established him. When he asked me to preface his book, I considered this as an appreciation from him. In this precious book which I highly recommend you, the man of God deals with this topic with tact, fineness, depth but also pertinence, topic where anthropology, sociology, psychology and the Word of God walk together in a perfect harmony. At the end of this book, the reader can only conclude that the Bible is really the Word of God, deals with everything, and is the solution

PREFACE

Past is Experience, Present is Experiment and the Future is Expectation. Dr. Eddy Kadiebu in his book "Overcoming the weight of the past," makes it very clear that God can make a New story out of your Old story and that can become your History.

Problems are intended to make us better not bitter. The author very skilfully illustrates through the lives of Job and Jacob that no problem leaves you where it found you.

Patience is Time Consuming but Anger is Life Consuming. Tempered by several years of ministerial experience, Apostle Eddy Kadiebu's insights on handling "Rejection" and "Guilt" are very relevant and compassionate. His practical suggestions are deeply Scripture based and would definitely bring about a transformation in the lives of the readers.

People will see themselves in the pages of this book through the authentic illustrations which vividly to the problems of this world, according to what Psalm 107:20 says: "He sent His word and healed them".

May God help you to find healing through this book and I would ask you a favour that is to invite as many people as possible to read this book. God bless you.

Roland Dalo
Pastor, founder of Centre Missionnaire Philadelphie RDC

Apostle Eddy Kadiebu Kandolo, whom I call "the Giant of Limoges", is giant, not only because of his physical size which constrains me to lift my head like a child to talk to him, but also because of the extraordinary dimension of his faith. There are those kinds of friendships that are built with time, but between Eddy and I, it was instantaneous for we have the same DNA. Apostle Eddy is a man of deep prayers. He will be an unavoidable voice in the French-speaking world in the near future. To preface his book is a great honour to me. Eddy is a doctor of the Word, but also a mighty evangelist and pastor, who, through his teachings and through his life, leads the flock to the right place: at the feet of the Good Shepherd. The reading and the study of his writings will inevitably affect you and strengthen you deeply.

Rémy BAYLE
Evangelist, founder of Action Mondiale Evangélisation
www.feuetgloire.com ; www.fete-evangile.com

DEDICATION

This book is dedicated to the memory of my dear uncle on my father's side, the Elder Kandolo Boniface, for everything I could get from him during my childhood.

You were for me a true father. Thank you for everything.

Apostle Eddy Kadiebu Kandolo

TO OVERCOME THE WEIGHT OF THE PAST THAT PURSUES YOU AND THAT CRUCHES YOU

CONTENTS

INTRODUCTION 17

1. THE THREE MAIN PERIODS OF THE EXISTENCE OF MAN 21

1.1 THE PAST 21
    1.1.1 To be weighed down by the past 22
    1.1.2 To learn the lessons from the past 27
    1.1.3 The true paradox between to forget and to remember 28

1.2 THE PRESENT 30

1.3 THE FUTURE 34

1.4 AN EVERLASTING FUTURE 35

GOD'S ANSWER TO OUR PROBLEM OF DISAPPOINTMENT 41

2.1 DEFINITIONS 41
    2.1.1 Definition of the word "answer" 41
    2.1.2 Definition of the word "disappointment" 43

2.2 A FEW SOURCES AND AREAS OF DISAPPOINTMENT IN LIFE 45

2.3 GOD ALLOWS DISAPPOINTMENTS 45
    2.3.1 Example 1: Job 46
    2.3.2 Example 2: Joseph 53

PARENTS' SINS AND MALEFICENT INHERITANCE: HOW TO GET OUT OF IT ? 55

3.1 THE SINS OF THE PARENTS 55
    3.1.1. Definition 55

    3.1.2 Solution: how to be delivered 59

3.2 THE POWER OF SATANIC HEREDITARY INHERITANCES 60
    3.2.1 Definition 62
    3.2.2 Areas in which they are manifested 62
    3.2.3 The properties of the notion of inheritance 63
    3.2.4 Solutions: how to be delivered? 64

GUILT AND FORGIVENESS TO OTHERS: A KEY STEP OF HEALING OF THE PAST 75

4.1 GUILT 75
    4.1.1. To acknowledge sin as sin 75
    4.1.2 The true confession 76
    4.1.3 Acceptation of God's forgiveness 78
    4.1.4 From forgiveness to liberation. 78
    4.1.5 The act of restitution 82

THE IMPACT OF CHILDHOOD IN ADULT LIFE 85

5.1 INTRODUCTION 85

5.2 SOME PRACTICAL EXAMPLES 87

5.3 GOD'S SOLUTION 89

THE SIN OF COMPARISON AND ITS CONSEQUENCES 93

6.1 DEFINITION AND CONSEQUENCES OF COMPARISON 96

6.2 SOLUTIONS 97

REJECTION AND ITS CONSEQUENCES IN ADULT LIFE 105

7.1 TO BECOME A FULFILLED ADULT AFTER HAVING BEEN A REJECTED CHILD 110

(Gideon, Joseph) 110
    7.1.1. Expression and consequences of rejection 110

7.1.2 God's solutions for restoration from rejection 112

7.2 YOU WERE NOT REJECTED BUT NOT WELL-LOVED 114
7.2.1 Solutions 115

GOD'S PROVISION TO PROBLEMS DUE TO THE IMPACT OF CHILDHOOD ON ADULT LIFE 121

8.1 MYSTERIES OF DIVINE PROVISION 121

8.2 GOD'S PRINCIPLES RELATED TO PROVISION 124
8.2.1 Provision is bound to God's presence in your life 124
8.2.2 God is the one who sovereignly determines the dimension of the provision you receive 125
8.2.3 God's grace, source of your provision 126
8.2.4 Trust the Provider rather than the provision 128
8.2.5 God is mighty and able to provide for your needs 129

TO TAKE SPIRITUALLY POSITION 131

TO OVERCOME THE WEIGHT OF THE PAST THAT PURSUES YOU AND THAT CRUCHES YOU

INTRODUCTION

"Do not remember the former things, nor consider the things of old. Behold, I will do a new thing, now it shall bring forth; shall you know it? I will even make a road in the wilderness and rivers in the desert." Isaiah 43:18-19

God promises new things. But in order to see the new things created, you need to go beyond the veil of realities. May God help us to see truly what is happening! He offers whoever wants to start it all again from the beginning the opportunity to do so. Failures are not accumulated for the Christian. At any time, he can talk about it to the Lord in prayer and experience a new departure with God, who never grows weary to give opportunities of change. Every christian can experience new departures in many areas of his life and thus move on from progress to progress.

"Do not fear, for you will not be ashamed; neither be disgraced for you will not be put to shame; for you will forget the shame of your youth and will not remember the reproach of your widowhood anymore. For your maker is your husband, the Lord of Hosts is His name; and your Redeemer is the Holy One of Israel; He is called the God of the whole earth." Isaiah 54:4-5

During the exile and the diaspora, Israel looks like a wife whose husband has repudiated, but this period is short compared to the everlasting blessing which the people will enjoy at the return of the Messiah who will gather the bride in tears. The sins of Israel resulted in his captivity in Egypt, the exile to Babylon and the current scattering, but the glory of the kingdom to come will be so great that it will eclipse the past failures.

During the exile and the scattering, Israel was reduced to nothing, despised like a woman unable to have children. The prophet led them to praise because of the promise given by the Lord of a fruitful future for his people, a restitution of the years devoured by the locusts and a restoration of a life devastated by a negative past.

Introduction

The Bible reveals to us the immensity of God's love for mankind. In order to help us to understand the intensity of this love and its implications, the prophets used marriage as a symbol of the relationship which unites God to his people.

It is interesting and significant to notice that marriage according to God is, first of all, a covenant and that, in this passage, God is referred to as the "husband of the people of Israel". When John the Baptist and Paul mention Jesus as the "husband" or the "only husband", they give him a title which belongs to God only, which confirms thus once more that Jesus is really God.

Israel is compared to a woman that has gone through hardships (times of suffering, of tears, and terrible afflictions). God tells her that her time of suffering is over. This is now time for comfort. God gives to Israel all guarantees of his protection and his faithfulness towards her; he adds this: *"Do not fear [...] your Maker is your husband." Isaiah 54:5*

Today, the Church is for Christ what Israel is for God. Christ works today for the Church to be what she ought to (be). All the promises God made to Israel become ours because of the Abrahamic covenant. Thus, God ensures in Christ Jesus a total restoration of life, concerning all kinds of aspects of our negative past which may crush and pursue us.

Apostle Paul says in Philippians 3:13-14:

"Brethren, I do not count myself to have apprehended; but one thing I do, forgetting those things which are behind and reaching forward to those things which are ahead, I press toward the goal for the prize of the upward call of God in Christ Jesus."

Christ chose Paul for the ultimate goal to model him on his glorious image and to make him his instrument. He who previously used to be a persecutor of the church with a disastrous past, he reduced the whole process of sanctification to one simple and clear objective to do "only one thing": to seek to conform himself to Christ. Thus, the believer must not rely on some works or successes of the past, nor dwell on his sins and failures. Allowing the past to take possession of oneself cuts down the efforts given to the present time.

CHAPTER 1

1. THE THREE MAIN PERIODS OF THE EXISTENCE OF MAN

The past is the time of memories, the present is the time of action, and the future the time for plans. It is important to manage these three phases of time appropriately and wisely. This will cause a peaceful mind and a well-regulated life.

As foretold, some people are weighed down by their past, waste their present with useless things and dreams of their future through the use of unrealistic and imaginary thoughts.

1.1 THE PAST

Apostle Paul wrote:

"Forgetting those things which are behind, and reaching forward those things which are ahead." Philippians 3:13

Indeed, as we will see it later, there is a kind of paradox which consists in, on one hand to forget, and on the other hand to remember. In fact, it deals with a state of mind, a way through which we look at things and experience them. The past may be a weight or a burden which crushes us, as well as it may become a source of blessing for the present and the future, when we learn the lessons.

According to the way we tackle this period of time, we will either have to put up with it as a hindrance in our daily life, or will use it as a springboard in order to go further. Thus, there are two possibilities: to be weighed down by our past, or to learn the lessons out of it.

1.1.1 To be weighed down by the past

Those who are weighed down by their past manifest at least two kinds of behaviours:

a) Those who live only of their memories:

Memories may be a good thing, as long as they do not become the constant focus of our thought, for sufficient for the day is its own trouble. In His goodness that is renewed every morning, God makes things new. It is good from time to time to look at the good memories of the past, but they must not be set on the table every single day.

Chap 1: The three main periods of the existence of man

There are those who are nostalgic from the glories of the past, who only live regretting the old victories, the past miracles, the success of old etc... Only this time was good, only their past was nice. Ecclesiastes 7:10 says:

"Do not say: "Why were the former days better than these?" For you do not inquire wisely concerning this."

To live only of our memories goes together with the risk not to be able to get rid of them anymore. Then we sever ourselves from a part of our personality and stay on what we already know, and we do not develop our potential. It is written in Numbers 11:4-6:

"Now the mixed multitude who were among them yielded to intense craving; so the children of Israel also wept again and said: who will give us meat to eat? We remember the fish which we ate freely in Egypt, the cucumbers, the melons, the leeks, the onions, and the garlic; but now our whole being is dried up; there is nothing at all except this manna before our eyes!"

The expression "mixed multitude" appears only here in the Old Testament. It refers to a mixed crowd of non-Israelites who had left Egypt with Israel at the Exodus time. The people started to regret the food they used to eat in Egypt, complaining presently to eat only manna. Despite they had physically left Egypt, they were still prisoners of it in their thoughts. Such is the case of many believers who enter salvation meanwhile they continue to focus on their negative past.

b) Those who are overwhelmed by the failures of the past:

Troubled with the past always in your mind, you often feel unable to build up your present and your future. Sometimes You feel misunderstood by the others, who seem not to understand why you cannot turn the page and move on.

The Bible, the Word of God, teaches us to offload our burdens. And in this area, there are two things we must get rid of: the bitterness caused by our failures and the guilt of our sins.

"Therefore, if anyone is in Christ, he is a new creation; old things have passed away; behold, all things have become new." 2 Corinthians 5:17

Let us fully accept God's forgiveness, in accordance with what is written.

"I, even I, am He who blots out your transgressions for my own sake; and I will not remember your sins." Isaiah 43:25

"For I will be merciful to their unrighteousness, and their sins and their lawless deeds I will remember no more." Hebrew 8:12

Chap 1: The three main periods of the existence of man

"If you, Lord, should mark iniquities, O Lord, who could stand?" Psalm 130:3

We can all have that confidence that we are forgiven for our sins, and justified, as it is declared in the Word of God:

"There is therefore now no condemnation for those who are in Christ Jesus." Romans 8:1

"Who shall bring a charge against God's elect? It is God who justifies. Who is he who condemns? It is Christ who died, and furthermore, is also risen, who is even at the right hand of God, who also makes intercession for us." Romans 8:33 (read from verses 28 to 39).

David the Psalmist says to God:

"I acknowledged my sin to you, and my iniquity I have not hidden. I said "I will confess my transgressions to the Lord", and you forgave the iniquity of my sin." Psalm 32:5

Let us receive through faith the forgiveness for our sins and let us enjoy the salvation of God in Jesus Christ:

"If we confess our sins, He is faithful and just to forgive us our sins and cleanse us from all unrighteousness." 1 John 1:9

With regards to our failures, if we can regret certain things for which we were responsible, we cannot go backwards. To recognize it has nothing to do with fatalism. In the contrary, there is a certain reality in the fact of admitting that we failed, in order to learn the lessons out of it. Let us not focus too long on the failure in itself but rather understand what caused it and which elements of our victory were missing. Jeremiah the prophet understood that to keep on thinking over bitter things of the past in his spirit would only hurt him, so he turned his thoughts to what gave him hope:

"Remember my affliction and roaming, the wormwood and the gall. My soul still remembers and sinks within me. This I recall to my mind, Therefore I have hope. Through the Lord's mercies we are not consumed because His compassions fail not. They are new every morning. Great is your faithfulness. "The Lord is my portion," says my soul, "therefore I hope in Him."" Lamentations 3:16-24

Every day, God gives his faithful love to his elected people. Like the manna in the desert, it is inexhaustible. This truth pushes Jeremiah to give praise. He is stunned by the continuous renewal of the grace of God that is offered to him. He understands now the infinite character of the faithful love of God and decides to wait for God's intervention in order to re-establish and bless his people, in spite of the circumstances.

1.1.2 To learn the lessons from the past

As we said before, the events of our past may either give us an incentive if it was a success, or cause us to reflect if it was a failure.

"And you shall remember that the Lord your God led you all the way these forty years in the wilderness, to humble you and test you, to know what was in your heart, whether you would keep his commandments or not." Deuteronomy 8:2

"Remember these, O Jacob, and Israel, for you are my servant; I have formed you, you are my servant; O Israel, you will not be forgotten by me."

"Remember! Do not forget how you provoked the Lord your God to wrath in the wilderness. From the day that you departed from the land of Egypt until you came to this place, you have been rebellious against the Lord." Deuteronomy 9:7

Therefore, there are some memories that encourage to prayer and to faith, and other that bring back on the ways of the Lord. Psalm 143:5 says:

"I remember the days of old; I meditate on all your works; I muse on the work of your hands. I spread out my hands to you; my soul longs for you like a thirsty land."

To remember the things of the past brings us to learn some lessons and to draw some conclusions. Failures of the past must give us wisdom, prudence, and bring some changes in our reasonings and behaviour, and lead us to a renewing of intelligence (Romans 12:2).

The success and the glories of the past must encourage us in our plans and struggles in the present.

The memories of the blessings received and even the divine punishment must lead us to be grateful and watchful people.

"Remember His marvellous works, which He has done, His wonders and the judgements of His mouth." 1 Chronicles 16:8-15

"Remember the former things of old, for I am God, and there is no other; I am God and there is none like me." Isaiah 46:9

1.1.3 The true paradox between to forget and to remember

With simple explanations we will try to show what appears paradoxal between to forget and to remember.

When we say "to forget" what is behind, the expression means that the past does not weigh us down anymore, even though we keep some painful times in memory, healing has come, as well as reconciliation, restoration, etc.

There is now therefore a kind of forgetfulness which consists in not allowing our past to weigh us down, and which allows us to remember enough, in order to remember the lessons and encouragements of our experiences in the past.

"Before I was afflicted I went astray, but now I keep Your Word." Psalm 119:67

To remember and to forget: this means that the reminder of the past may be useful, yet it must not become a burden that crushes, nor like a matter of glory which holds our attention, immobilizes us and prevents us from excelling.

To be fully in the present, to foresee the future... For some it is very complicated. And this difficulty prevents them from developing their potential and from moving forward in life. We will try to go in deep about this in the following chapters in order to reveal the keys that are necessary to fully enjoy the present and above all to well foresee the future.

1.2 THE PRESENT

The present is this very fugitive instant of every minute and even every second of our life. Words I just wrote are already part of the past!

The present is the time for action, where every decision will impact the future. The present is today, every day during which we are at work, either for ourselves, or for the Lord. The Psalmist was praying to God saying:

"So teach us to number our days, that we may gain a heart of wisdom." Psalm 90:12

A proverb says: *"Do not postpone tomorrow what you can already do today."* And the Ecclesiastes wrote:

"Whatever your hand finds to do, do it with your might; for there is no work or device or knowledge or wisdom in the grave where you are going." Ecclesiastes 9:10

Today is the right time to start something without waiting, to seize the opportunities that are given to us, for tomorrow does not belong to us but is in God's hands.

"Whereas you do not know what will happen tomorrow! For what is your life? It is even a vapor that appears for a little time, and then vanishes away." James 4:14

Chap 1: The three main periods of the existence of man

"For I considered all this in my heart, so that I could declare it all; that the righteous and the wise and their works are in the hand of God. People know neither love nor hatred by anything they see before them." Ecclesiastes 9:1

We can use our own measure to calculate the speed with which times goes by today, but God does not use the same measure.

"For a thousand years in your sight are like yesterday when it is past, and like a watch in the night." Psalm 90:4

"With the Lord one day is as a thousand years, and a thousand years as one day." 2 Peter 3:8

For us, time goes by quickly, therefore we must not waste it.

The difference in the achievement of exploits in life with God is also determined by the way which (that) people use their time. Although God has given different spiritual gifts and talents to all his children, he gave them all the same number of hours every day.

It is written in Ephesians 5:16-17:

"Redeeming the time, because the days are evil. Therefore do not be unwise, but understand what the will of the Lord is."

Today, this is the time of the grace of God for all, as it was for Zacchaeus:

"When Jesus came to the place, He looked up and saw him, and said to him, "Zacchaeus, make haste and come down, for today, I must stay at your house."" Luke 19:5

"Jesus said to him, "Today salvation has come to this house, because he also is a son of Abraham."" Luke 19:9

God has established a favourable time which is prolonged and which is called "day of salvation":

"For He says: "In an acceptable time I have heard you, and in the day of salvation I have helped you."" 2 Corinthians 6:2

For every human being there is a day where God calls him to give him grace and to save him, a favourable day to accept God's salvation, according to what is written in the Bible.

"Therefore, as the Holy Spirit says: "Today, if you will hear His voice, do not harden your hearts."" Hebrew 3:7

« *The Lord is not slack concerning His promise, as some count slackness, but is long-suffering toward us, not willing that any should perish but that all should come to repentance.* » 2 Peter 3 :8-9

The present is also the day that we recommend to God for our daily needs, as the Lord Jesus teaches:

« *Give us day by day our daily bread.* » Luke 11 :3

Chap 1: The three main periods of the existence of man

« *Therefore do not worry about tomorrow, for tomorrow will worry about its own things. Sufficient for the day is its own trouble.* » *Matthew 6 :34*

This does not prevent our daily job from providing for the following days and even years, for example with systems of retirement that do not disagree with the will of God, on the contrary:

« *Go to the ant, you sluggard! Consider her ways and be wise, which, having no captain, overseer or ruler, provides her supplies in the summer, and gather the food in the harvest.* » *Proverbs 6:6-8*

There are things that need to be renewed every day: the meal of yesterday is not enough for the next day. Every morning, we get up and get ready to go about our business. Every morning, God renews his goodness.

« *Through the Lord's mercies we are not consumed because His compassions fail not. They are new every morning. Great is your faithfulness. "The Lord is my portion," says my soul, "therefore I hope in Him."" Lamentations 3:22-23*

Every day the Lord gives us His grace and His support.

"Oh, satisfy us early with your mercy, that we may rejoice and be glad all our days!" Psalm 90:14

Every day we must seek God and walk with Him.

1.3 THE FUTURE

Tomorrow is the time of plans, of hope, but also the time of uncertainty. We cannot know what is going to happen tomorrow.

"Whereas you do not know what will happen tomorrow! For what is your life? It is even a vapor that appears for a little time, and then vanishes away." James 4:14

In spite of our precarious future on this earth, we must yet anticipate and make plans.

« How long will you slumber, O sluggard? When will you rise from your sleep? A little sleep, a little slumber, a little folding of the hands to sleep – so shall poverty come on you like a prowler, and your need like an armed man. » Proverbs 6:8-11

Concerning our plans, it is important to know that, in spite of all our wisdom and diligence, they do not depend on us only.

"The preparations of the heart belong to man, but the answer of the tongue is from the Lord." Proverbs 16:1

"There are many plans in a man's heart, nevertheless the Lord's counsel – that will stand." Proverb 19:21

This is why we are encouraged to entrust everything to the Lord:

"Commit your works to the Lord, and your thoughts will be established." Proverbs 16:3

"Commit your way to the Lord, trust also in Him, and He shall bring it to pass." Psalm 37:5

"Be anxious for nothing, but in everything by prayer and supplication, with thanksgiving, let your requests be made known to God." Philippians 4:6

"Casting all your cares upon Him, for He cares for you." 1 Peter 5:7

We can thus say together with the psalmist that our future is in God's hands.

"But as for me, I trust in you, O Lord; I say, "You are my God." My times are in your hands." Psalm 31:14-15

1.4 AN EVERLASTING FUTURE

For those who believe in the Lord Jesus Christ, tomorrow is the time of hope, the time for which they trust God for their everlasting future.

"For me, I will look to the Lord; I will wait for the God of my salvation; My God will hear me." Micah 7:7

As we have said before, when we trust God, we are confident for the next day for our earthly life. Nevertheless, there is a much more important future, which God urges us to consider. Jesus gave a parable to teach us the reality of the future.

"Then He spoke a parable to them, saying: "The ground of a certain rich man yielded plentifully. And he thought within himself, saying, "What shall I do, since I have no room to store my crops?" So he said, "I will do this: I will pull down my barns and will build greater, and there I will store all my crops and my goods. And I will say to my soul, "Soul, you have many goods laid up for many years; take your ease; eat, drink, and be merry." But God said to him, "Fool! This night your soul will be required of you; then whose will those things be which you have provided? So is he who lays up treasures for himself, and is not rich toward God." Luke 12:16-21

Somewhere else, Jesus insists on what should be our priority:

"Seek first the Kingdom of God and His righteousness, and all these things shall be added to you." Matthew 6:33

Those who are not regenerated focus on material things. They even create false gods in the vain hope that these will help them in their various needs and requests, but these gods are nothing else than the projection of wicked men and perverse demons, sly, selfish, violent, untrustworthy, indifferent, capricious, ruthless. Far from being able to hope for any help from these gods, the best they can do is to calm them down.

Contrary to those lifeless pagan divinities, in His omniscience, our heavenly Father knows that we need those material things which the non-regenerated people are looking for. And He not only knows it, but He is also compassionate and possesses unlimited resources and capacities to meet His children's needs. The good fatherhood of God cancels all kinds of legitimate worry or fear or anxiety. Paradoxically, believers do not obtain the things they need while they are looking for them. They receive them indirectly if they seek for God's kingdom, for all these things will be added to them. In other words, our focus must not be on food, clothes, money, houses, cars, or any other material goods, but rather on worship, service and proclamation of the Gospel of Christ, a way to live in obedience to the Word, looking for the truth, for holiness, and for love. The burning interest of the believer's life must be centred on the kingdom of God, on the sphere of salvation in which God reigns as king and master. Everything must be done for the honour and the expansion of Christ's lordship. Christian life starts with repentance, self-denial, humility, sadness because of sin, as well as with a hunger and thirst which follow the saving faith; this results in a life of worship, of service and obedience. Jesus promised, to those whose soul is seeking for the glories of the kingdom, that they would see that God answers to their earthly needs. Apostle Paul specifies one thing which concerns all those who belong to Christ:

"For our citizenship is in Heaven, from which we also eagerly wait for the Saviour, The Lord Jesus Christ, who will transform our lowly body that it may be conformed to His glorious body, according to the working by which He is able to subdue all things to Himself." Philippians 3:20-21

He said this in opposition to those who were placing their hope and pleasure only in the earthly things.

"For many walk, of whom I have told you often, and now tell you even weeping, that they are the enemies of the cross of Christ: whose end is destruction, whose god is their belly, and whose glory is in their shame – who set their mind on earthly things." Philippians 3:18-19

Those who do not know the Lord are hopeless. They think that their future is ended at their death, so they behave in this world without worrying about eternity. They say, *"Let us eat and drink, let us take pleasure now, for tomorrow we will die."* (2 Corinthians 15:32)

The Gentiles too walk according to the futility of their mind, having their understanding darkened, being alienated from the life of God, because of the ignorance that is in them, because of the blindness of their heart; who, being past feeling, have given themselves over to lewdness, to work all uncleanness with greediness (Ephesians 4:17-19). For us who are saved, let us consider things through God's point of view, for if we cannot bring the past back, we can live the present while doing righteousness in the faith in the Lord Jesus Christ, the eyes set towards the future which we expect.

"How you turned to God from idols to serve the living and true God, and to wait for His Son from heaven, whom He raised from the dead, Jesus who delivers us from the wrath to come." 1 Thessalonians 1:9-10

To conclude this chapter, I leave you with this comforting word in all situations of our life:

"Jesus Christ is the same yesterday, today and forever." Hebrew 13:8

TO OVERCOME THE WEIGHT OF THE PAST THAT PURSUES YOU AND THAT CRUCHES YOU

CHAPTER 2
GOD'S ANSWER TO OUR PROBLEM OF DISAPPOINTMENT

2.1 DEFINITIONS

For a start, let us define the two key words of this chapter for a good understanding.

2.1.1 Definition of the word "answer"

This word may have several meanings:

- What somebody says, writes, or does in order to answer: for instance: "Answer from the accused to the question of the judge.

- Solution, explanation, clarification, brought to some question, to some obscure point. For ex.: this problem has not found any answer.

- Action in response to an attack, to criticism, for ex.: This implication requires a response.
- Behaviour or feeling in response / in return: For ex. My affection remained without response.
- Somebody's response to a call: For ex.: I knock, but no answer.

It is written in Jeremiah 33:3:

"Call to me, and I will answer you, and show you great and mighty things, which you do not know."

The chapter 33 of Jeremiah follows the one from chapter 32 where Jeremiah was still in the court of the prison (see ch.32:1-2). God reminded Jeremiah both His power and character as the God who made the earth (See ch.32:17) revealing to Jeremiah His name (Yahweh, God emphasized on His faithfulness to keep His covenant with the people. Jeremiah did not understand how God could re-establish a nation who was destined to judgement. So God exhorted the prophet to call upon Him in order to understand. God promised to answer him and to reveal him great things, hidden things[1]. God's plans in disappointment are imperceptible to the natural man. Only God can unveil the divine goals behind every disappointment.

---

[1] Hidden things : Litteral translation of the French version of Jeremiah 33 :3 – Segond révisée 1979

He would communicate to Jeremiah the truths concerning Israel's future, which(that) the prophet ignored or did not catch. There is a divine answer to every single disappointment (that) we go through.

2.1.2 Definition of the word "disappointment"

Disappointment: state or feeling of a disappointed person, deceived in her expectation. A person or a thing may be the origin of this feeling.

In the biblical text of Genesis 41:8-16, the joint analysis of Pharaoh's counsellors and the professionals of the dream called in his presence resulted only in a disappointment, for none of them could provide an exact interpretation. They did not know that they were preparing the place for the introduction of Joseph in the Egyptian story. Joseph's interpretation turned the minds on what God had decided for Egypt. After having interpreted the dream, Joseph explained to Pharaoh how to survive during the next fourteen years. It was incongruous for a man both slave and prisoner to suggest a long-term strategy to store reserves in order to provide for the needs in the future. Famines had already devastated Egypt before, but this time, the divine warning allowed serious and sustained preparations. Denying his own competence, Joseph warned Pharaoh from the beginning that the answer he was expecting could only come from God.

The Bible declares in the book of Job 1:20-22:

"Then, Job arose, tore his robe, and shaved his head; and he fell to the ground and worshiped. And he said: "Naked I came from my mother's womb, and naked I shall return there. The Lord gave, and the Lord has taken away; blessed be the name of the Lord." In all this Job did not sin nor charged God with wrong."

Job's disappointment was Satan's work in the permissive will of God, but became God's plan to lead Job to spiritual maturity. He became a man who accepted God's sovereignty not with resignation but joyfully, being able to say even after the suffering: "I know that You can do everything, and that no purpose of Yours can be withheld from You."

Through suffering, he went from the step of hearing God to the step of seeing God, from the step of boasting freely about his own righteousness in all the aspects of his life to the step of condemning himself and repenting with humility.

If we are looking for solutions to the problems of disappointment, we must find the answers offered by God and lay aside those offered by man. We must look at what God is doing and adopt His point of view.

2.2 A FEW SOURCES AND AREAS OF DISAPPOINTMENT IN LIFE

We may go through disappointments in the following areas of our life:

- Affective life
- Professional
- Relationships
- Spiritual...

The sources may be of different kinds:

- Unachieved expectations
- The lack of achievement of the plans
- The lack of answer to a prayer,
- The dissatisfaction in various areas of investment (ministry, business, family, education, profession, social...)

2.3 GOD ALLOWS DISAPPOINTMENTS

There is no disappointment that happens to a child of God without being authorized or allowed by God. The devil and all his agents may initiate the events that lead to disappointment, yet the devil cannot touch children of God without God's permission. No matter how great the disappointment is, bear in mind that YHWH is He who makes all things to work together for the good to those who love Him. Two biblical examples illustrate this well:

2.3.1 Example 1: Job

"Now there was a day when his sons and daughters were eating and drinking wine in their oldest brother's house; and a messenger came to Job and said, "The oxen were plowing and the donkeys feeding beside them, when the Sabeans raided them and took them away—indeed they have killed the servants with the edge of the sword; and I alone have escaped to tell you!" While he was still speaking, another also came and said, "The fire of God fell from heaven and burned up the sheep and the servants, and consumed them; and I alone have escaped to tell you!" While he was still speaking, another also came and said, "The Chaldeans formed three bands, raided the camels and took them away, yes, and killed the servants with the edge of the sword; and I alone have escaped to tell you!" While he was still speaking, another also came and said, "Your sons and daughters were eating and drinking wine in their oldest brother's house, and suddenly a great wind came from across the wilderness and struck the four corners of the house, and it fell on the young people, and they are dead; and I alone have escaped to tell you!" Then Job arose, tore his robe, and shaved his head; and he fell to the ground and worshiped. And he said: "Naked I came from my

mother's womb, and naked shall I return there. The LORD gave, and the LORD has taken away; blessed be the name of the LORD." In all this Job did not sin nor charge God with wrong."

There are six important things I would like to clarify for our good understanding:

1. We can see that God allowed Satan to do all this to Job. But He also determined the boundary which Satan was not authorized to cross: Job himself could not be touched. In all circumstances of disappointment, God sets the limits which Satan cannot overstep, for He knows our faith, our strength and our weaknesses. We can then believe that in spite of our disappointments, in His love, God keeps us in safety. Satan cannot touch the believer's life if he is not allowed to do so by God in his permissive or original will.

2. Job's state of mind. He was not the kind of man living in sin and whom God could have punished using the devil to do so (Job 1:5; 31:1-2; 31:9:10; 31:16-23; 31:29-32). On the contrary, Job was upright and righteous in all his ways. Yet God allowed Satan to afflict him. The question is then to understand why God allowed it. Disappointments are not all the systematic consequences of sin or a punishment. God makes everything for a purpose.

A pure soul is not immune to disappointment, because God allows disappointment also in the life of the righteous one, in order to reach some specific purposes. It is a mistake to think that every disappointment that happens in life is the punishment of sin.

3. Job knew God but this knowledge of God had not reached maturity yet. For he said after his disappointments:

"I have heard of You by the hearing of the ear, but now my eye sees You." Job 42:5

As we already underlined it previously, Job went from the step of hearing God to the step of seeing Him. This disappointment, that was the work of the enemy in the permissive will of God, became God's plan for Job. He could then say that he understood God after having seen Him with the eye of faith. Never before had he so well realized the greatness, the majesty, the sovereignty and the independence of God.

4. Disappointment was allowed in Job's life in order to lead him both to spiritual maturity and to a deeper communion with God.

Behind every disappointment there is a purpose God wants to attain. Now Job knew that God was far beyond the first ideas he had of Him before, due to his ignorance at that time. Through disappointment Job was led to a personal confrontation with God, putting an end to all his reasonings and inspiring him a great respect. With the new discerning acquired about God's ways and character, His might, and His creative genius, His sovereignty, His providential concern and love, Job admitted his own unworthiness and repented. His declaration "I abhor myself" means that he rejected the accusations he had made against God in his pride.

God had already rebuked Job for the accusations and condemnations he had made against God (Job 40:2). Job repented then in dust and ashes, which was a way to express his shame (according to Genesis 18:27). To throw dust in the air for it to fall on one's head or putting some over the body was showing that the person was humbling (according to Isaiah 58:5 and Daniel 9:3). In the past, Job had deplored his losses, but here he was deploring his sin. Quite obviously, he did not repent of the sins which his three friends had imagined, and he persisted to declare that his suffering was not resulting from sins committed before all this happened (Job 27:2-6). However, as Elihu had said, bitterness and pride had followed the loss of his riches, his family members, his health (Job 32:2; 33:17; 35:12-13; 36:9; 37:24). In the beginning, Job's response was appropriate (Job 1:21-22; 2:10). Now, Job could see what God had shown to him (Job 40:5), that is, that no one could make any accusation against Him. Aware that God had no duty towards man, Job put an end to his questions and bitterness. Now Job was satisfied with what God had revealed about himself, even though he had not revealed anything about his own troubles. Since then, Job was ready to trust the sovereign God, whose ways are perfect (Psalm 18:31), even without understanding them. Undoubtedly God forgave Him his previous pride.

It is then important to consult the Lord to understand His language behind every disappointment. What does He want to teach you?

It is also interesting to consider that, in life, it is not so much the disappointment that is problematic. It is rather the attitude we adopt that will determine either our victory or our failure. It is the attitude of faith in God's love that will make all things work together for the good of those who love him.

"Job answered the Lord and said: "I know that You can do everything, and that no purpose of Yours can be withheld from You. You asked "Who is this who hides counsel

without knowledge?" Therefore, I have uttered what I did not understand, things too wonderful for me, which I did not know. Listen, please, and let me speak; You said, "I will question you and you will answer Me". "I have heard of You by the hearing of the ear, but now my eye sees You. Therefore, I abhor myself, and repent in dust and ashes." Job 42:1-6

Job became a man who is aware of and recognizes God's sovereignty, not by resignation but accepted it joyfully. The perfect God found in Job a righteous man who was not yet perfect in his union with Him. He used disappointment and afflictions to make him a perfect man after His heart, in all areas.

5. **Self-denial** (Luke 9:23; 1 John 2:15-17). God's will for all those who belong to Him is that they deny themselves, that they take up their cross every day and follow Him to this place where the "self's life" is crucified, where the desire to be loved, honoured, is put to death, as well as the love of the world and of the things of the world.

Therefore, when we look at what we could not be or possess or experience, it is important to check, whether it was for our own glory or for the glory of God.

6. To make sure that we love God and that we are called according to His purpose (Romans 8:28).

   "And we know that all things work together for good to those who love God, to those who are the called according to His purpose."

   If we are confident in these two things, God will use everything that may happen to us for our good, no matter the troubles, betrayals, persecutions, failures, enemies, shut doors, rejections, and blocks. In short, every situation may occur; anyway, God will make all of them to work together for good to those who love Him and who are the called according to His purpose. We must understand that nothing will happen to us without being first allowed by God, our heavenly Father who loves us. We must also bear in mind that God will work for our good everything He allows to happen in our life. In His providence, He leads every single event of our life, even suffering, temptation and disappointment, for our own benefit, both temporal, and eternal.

   "The Lord brings the counsel of the nations to nothing; He makes the plans of the peoples of no effect. The counsel of the Lord stands forever, the plans of His heart to all generations." Psalm 33:10-11

The Psalmist talks about the power of the Lord in History. God's purposes overthrow those of the Gentiles. His plans are achieved in spite of all that men can do. Assuredly a God with such mighty Word and works deserves to be celebrated.

God is not the author of all things, yet He governs over all things. He is able in His sovereignty to use anything that happens. He incorporates every event in His great plan for His own. No matter the other's motives, when we fully trust Him in the midst of disappointment, He filters everything through His fatherly love for us.

2.3.2 Example 2: Joseph

"Then his brothers also went and fell down before his face, and they said, "Behold, we are your servants." Joseph said to them, "Do not be afraid, for am I in the place of God? But as for you, you meant evil against me; but God meant it for good, in order to bring it about as it is this day, to save many people alive. Now therefore, do not be afraid; I will provide for you and your little ones." And he comforted them and spoke kindly to them. Genesis 50:18-21

Joseph's brothers had meditated evil against him but God changed it into good. Finally, the bad intentions did not prevail over him. Rather God's plans prevailed for him (Isaiah 14:24-27).

"The Lord of hosts has sworn it, saying, "Surely, as I have thought, so it shall come to pass, and as I have purposed, so it shall stand. [...] For the Lord of hosts has purposed, and who will annul it? His hand is stretched out, and who will turn it back?"

Therefore, no matter our disappointments, the Lord uses it for our good, as long as we love Him and are called according to His purpose. Our disappointments are springboards that propel us into God's purposes.

CHAPTER 3

PARENTS' SINS AND MALEFICENT INHERITANCE: HOW TO GET OUT OF IT ?

3.1 THE SINS OF THE PARENTS

3.1.1. Definition

"You shall not bow down to them nor serve them. For I, the Lord your God, am a jealous God, visiting the iniquity of the fathers upon the children to the third and fourth generations of those who hate Me, but showing mercy to thousands, to those who love Me and keep My commandments. You shall not take the name of the Lord your God in vain, for the Lord will not hold him guiltless who takes his name in vain." Exodus 20:5-7

Some people endure not only the consequences of their sins, but also suffer because of their parents' sins, grandparents, great-grandparents and ancestors etc...

"And the Lord passed before him and proclaimed, "The Lord, the Lord God, merciful and gracious, long-suffering, and abounding in goodness and truth, keeping mercy for thousands, forgiving iniquity and transgression and sin, by no means clearing the guilty, visiting the iniquity of the fathers upon the children and the children's children to the third and the fourth generation." Exodus 34:6-7

The strange conduct of some people may result from God's judgement upon them because of the sins of their ancestors. They endure the consequences of the sins which they have somehow inherited. Certain tribes, families, countries etc... are bound by such and such behaviour. You can notice some unexplainable anomalies in your character or in your personality. In your own behaviour, there may be some things that are completely in disharmony with the rest of your personality and behaviour. Generally, this results from the sins of your ancestors for which you still endure the consequences.

Some of these consequences are related to national or tribal tendencies that are manifest in some negative aspects of the character and are generally associated to certain nations, tribes, races, etc. For example, some categories of people may be characterized by roughness, laziness, anger, greediness, drunkenness, immorality, implacability, polygamy, gluttony etc. You must carefully examine what is the fundamental defect of your race, your tribe, your culture and get rid of it in the name of Jesus Christ. If you don't do it, you may remain captive from them. The question we may ask then is to know whether or not children are punished for the sins of their parents. The answer is no, they are not, nor the parents for the sins of their children. Everyone is responsible for their own sins. Ezekiel 18:20 says:

"The soul who sins shall die. The son shall not bear the guilt of the father, nor the father bear the guilt of the son."

This verse states clearly that the chastening for the sins of somebody is fully endured by him/her. However, there is another verse that pushed some people to believe that the Bible teaches an intergenerational chastening for sins, but this is an erroneous interpretation. This verse is in Exodus 20:5 which we already quoted and which was referring to idols:

"You shall not bow down to them nor serve them. For I, the Lord your God, am a jealous God, visiting the iniquity

of the fathers upon the children to the third and fourth generations of those who hate Me."

Here it is not about punishment of sin but about its consequences. This means that the consequences of the sin of a man may also have an influence on the next generations. God was saying to the Israelites that their children would feel the impact of the generation of their parents as a natural result from their disobedience and hatred towards God. Children raised in such an environment would practice the same idolatry, falling in the same identical and preestablished scenario of disobedience.

The disobedience of one generation would obviously cause to root sin so deeply that many generations would be necessary to invert the process. God does not hold us responsible of the sins of our parents, but sometimes we suffer from their consequences, according to Exodus 20:5.

As stated in Ezekiel 18:20, we are responsible for our own sins and we must suffer the chastening for it. We cannot share our sin with somebody else, nor could anybody else be held responsible for it. Only one man bore the sins of others and paid the debt for all so that sinners may become perfectly righteous and pure before God. This man is Jesus Christ. God sent Jesus into this world in order to exchange His perfection for our sins.

"For He made Him who knew no sin to be sin for us, that we might become the righteousness of God." 2 Corinthians 5:21

Jesus Christ removes from whoever comes to Him in faith every punishment for the sins committed.

3.1.2 Solution: how to be delivered

Daniel (Daniel 9:4-14) and Nehemiah (Nehemiah 1:5-7) bore on them the sins of their people and made them their own sins. They bore them before God in the prayer of confession and besought God's mercy. He heard them and forgave them and the people. To be practical:

1. **Confess their sins,** making sure that you already dealt with your personal sins and made an act of restitution. For it is useless to seek to solve the problem of the consequences of the sins of ancestors without putting an end to a sinful life. This confession will not lead them to Heaven but will make you free from these consequences, since you are the one who suffers.

2. It is important **to get rid of bitterness and resentment** which you had shown to your ancestors further to what they had done, for the following reasons.

a) If you keep your bitterness, you are the one who suffers, not them.

b) This may be transmitted to your children

c) This will be an obstacle to your prayer to God

d) This will end up with creating trouble in your health

3. **Release with the prayer of faith** all those who are alive and still suffer from the consequences of these sins. Ask the Holy Spirit to reveal you the members of your family that are captive because of these sins of your ancestors. Once for all cancel all the tendencies to do evil in the future. Ask the Lord to remove every consequence on your children or any member of your family.

3.2 THE POWER OF SATANIC HEREDITARY INHERITANCES

"And Jehoshaphat rested with his fathers, and was buried with his fathers in the City of David his father. Then Jehoram his son reigned in his place. Ahaziah the son of Ahab became king over Israel in Samaria in the seventeenth year of Jehoshaphat king of Judah, and reigned two years over Israel. He did evil in the sight of the Lord, and walked in the way of his mother and in the way of Jeroboam the son of Nebat, who made Israel sin; for he served Baal and worshiped him, and provoked the Lord God of Israel to

Chap 3: Parents' sins and maleficent inheritance: how to get out of it?

anger, according to all that his father had done." 1 Kings 22:50-53

"[...] Israel, with whom the Lord had a covenant and charged them, saying: "You shall not fear other gods, nor bow down to them nor serve them nor sacrifice to them; but the Lord, who brought you up from the land of Egypt with great power and an outstretched arm, Him you shall fear, Him you shall worship, and to Him you shall offer sacrifice. And the statutes, the ordinances, the law, and the commandment which he wrote for you, you shall be careful to observe forever; you shall not fear other gods. And the covenant that I have made with you, you shall not forget, nor shall you fear other gods. But the Lord your God you shall fear; and He will deliver you from the hand of your enemies." However they did not obey, but they followed their former rituals. So these nations feared the Lord, yet served their carved images; also their children and their children's children have continued doing as their fathers did, even to this day." 2 Kings 17:35-41

"Thus says the Lord: For three transgressions of Judah, and for four, I will not turn away its punishment, because they have despised the law of the Lord, and have not kept His commandments. Their lies lead them astray, lies which their fathers followed." Amos 2:4

Matthew 14:1-12 (Herodias's influence on her daughter with regards to the death of John the Baptist.)

3.2.1 Definition

The satanic hereditary deposit consists in all the results of consecration and spiritual maleficent inheritance which have become now a slavery that limits your success in normal life. Let us start first with a definition of "inheritance".

The inheritance is defined as the patrimony acquired or transmitted by right of succession, which we hold from a predecessor. This is also what we inherit from a previous generation with regards to the character, ideology, etc...

3.2.2 Areas in which they are manifested

a)**Spiritual** (occult consultations, instability, pacts with Satan...)

b)**Feelings** (Devilish feelings, hatred, jealousy, bitterness, lack of forgiveness, grudge...)

c)**Affective** (Bond of single life, family divisions, lack of brotherly affection...)

d)**Social** (Blocks, regression, repeated failures, poverty, drunkenness, instability, mediocrity...)

e)**Physical** (Hereditary diseases, incurable diseases, malformation...)

When we come to Christ, we are enlightened and we must live our life in the light of the Scriptures,

Chap 3: Parents' sins and maleficent inheritance: how to get out of it?

to discern if we have not inherited a satanic deposit, and to pray according to what we can notice in our life, under the direction and leadership of the Holy Spirit.

3.2.3 The properties of the notion of inheritance

It is about a relationship on four axes (see the illustrations below).

1. Transitivity: If B inherits from A and if C inherits from B, then C inherits from A.

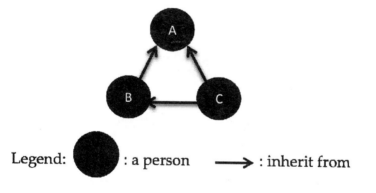

2. No reflexivity: a class (or a person) cannot inherit from itself. It cannot make a return on itself, nor take itself for object (someone else). A cannot inherit from himself/herself.

3. No symmetry: If A inherit from B, B does not inherit from A.

4. No cycle: It is not possible for B to inherit from A, for C to inherit from B, and for A to inherit from C.

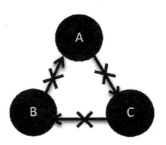

3.2.4 Solutions: how to be delivered?

a) To break the power of satanic inheritances

Christ came to destroy the works of the devil.

"He who sins is of the devil, for the devil has sinned from the beginning. For this purpose the Son of God was manifested, that He might destroy the works of the devil." 1 John 3:8

In Him, every curse is changed into blessing, for He took upon Himself our curse through the death of the cross, so that all those who accept His sacrifice be liberated from the power of the curse. In this context, the expression englobes a series of activities of the devil: sin, rebellion, temptation, government of the world, persecution, and accusations against the saints Christ came to destroy the works of the devil (1 John 3:8). The expression englobes a series of activities of the devil: sin, rebellion, temptation, government of the world, persecution, and accusations against the saints.

b) Seek first the crux of the problem and its related effects

Many seek to solve superficially the problems that are due to the power of satanic hereditary inheritances dealing with the problem superficially, which is a fatal error. Whereas it is sometimes of major importance to know and to understand the centre of the problem and its associated effects in order to solve it in deep.

You can pray and ask God to enlighten you by the Holy Spirit, for there are situations that require to be dealt with at the root and specific prayers.

Allow the Word of God to enlighten you.

"He declares His word to Jacob, His statutes and His judgements to Israel." Psalm 147:19,

"The Lord opens the eyes of the blind; the Lord raises those who are bowed down; the Lord loves the righteous." Psalm 146:8

c) *To renounce the bounds and get out of the satanic prison: to take position spiritually.*

If you are not fed up with a spiritual situation which crushes you, you will not have the will and determination to get out of it. And the renouncements by faith are also important, relying on the strength and the power of God, to cause you to step out of all kinds of satanic prison.

Faith in the Word of God must push us to realize who we are in Jesus. This awareness, as well as the realization of both what we become in Jesus and what we spiritually become in Christ re-position us.

"And immediately the man was made well, took up his bed, and walked. And that day was the Sabbath. The Jews therefore said to him who was cured, "It is the Sabbath; it is not lawful to carry your bed." He answered them, He who made me well said to me "Take up your bed and walk"." John 5:9-11

This man had a choice: he could either let the Jews' accusations condemn him concerning his healing on Sabbath Day and then remain paralyzed, or by faith, he could also seize the word of Jesus about him ("Take up your bed and walk"). This pushed him first to change the thought he had of himself before remaining paralyzed, to then stand up and walk, experiencing thus the power of divine healing.

To take his bed and to stand up was for this man a way to take spiritually position with regards to his bond and to the satanic prison in which he was slave.

The lack of renouncement and the lack of spiritual stand cause many to remain in satanic bondage.

"But someone will say, "You have faith, and I have works." Show me your faith without your work, and I will show you my faith with my works. You believe that there is one God. You do well. Even the demons believe – and tremble! But do you want to know, O foolish man, that faith without works is dead? Was not Abraham justified by works when he offered Isaac his son on the altar? Do you see that faith was working together with his works, and by works faith was made perfect? And the Scripture was fulfilled which says, "Abraham believed God, and it was accounted to him for righteousness." James 2 :18-23

d) **Refuse to accept what the devil is author as a normal reality.**

When he is at work in somebody's life, the devil makes sure that he goes unnoticed, for this way, he is more efficient in his destructive work. In our subconscious, he either makes thoughts and acts out to be our own, or he causes us to believe that everything that is happening in our life is something normal. Refuse everything which the devil comes to impose on you as a reality, leaning on the Word of God that is the truth able to change realities (Ephesians 5:10-11 *"Finding out what is acceptable to the Lord. And have no fellowship with the unfruitful works of darkness, but rather expose them."*). The Word of God has the power to change all reality imposed by the enemy for it is the truth. It produces in us the faith that is needed, that is neither unaware of the reality nor limited by it. What God says about you must happen in the physical, no matter the reality you face.

e) **To get rid of all kinds of evil example in the family**

"You shall not bow down to them, nor serve them. For I, the Lord your God, am a jealous God, visiting the iniquity of the fathers upon the children to the third or fourth generations of those who hate Me, but showing mercy to thousands, to those who love Me and keep My commandments." Deuteronomy 5:9-10

In this text, God announces to His people the consequences of the sins of the parents on the next generations. The example of Guehazi in 2 Kings 5:27 illustrates it well:

"Therefore the leprosy of Naaman shall cling to you and your descendants forever." And he went out from his presence leprous, as white as snow." 2 Kings 5:27

Many people glorify themselves for some evil inheritances of the family about their character, behaviour, attitudes or some devilish services manifested in the family. To accept them is a way to give an access to the enemy and allow him to continue his work of destruction.

"Christ has redeemed us from the curse of the law, having become a curse for us (for it is written "Cursed is everyone who hangs on a tree.)" Galatians 3:13

The Greek word for "redeem" was often used for the purchase of a slave's liberty or from a debtor. Christ's death served as a substitution for sin, and therefore it could satisfy God's righteousness and put an end to his wrath, so that we can actually say that Christ redeemed the believers from bondage of sin and from condemnation to eternal death, which they were destined to. By taking upon Him on the cross the wrath of God against the sins of the believer Christ took the curse that was resting on those who broke the law, and thus, he cancelled the rights which the enemy used to have on man because of sin.

f) *Every damage caused to your destiny by maleficent inheritance must be repaired in Jesus' name* (Joel 2:25).

God promises to restore every damage done by the enemy to our destiny in repositioning us in our divine inheritance, as heir and joint-heir with Christ. Thus, with faith, we can pray and ask him the full restoration in all areas that had been destroyed by the enemy.

Let us highlight that God's forgiveness, obtained through Jesus, breaks the power of the accuser. Even though certain things result from our ignorance in the past, in His father's love, God is able to restore us in His compassion.

"So I will restore to you the years that the swarming locust has eaten, the crawling locust, the consuming locust and the chewing locust, My great army which I sent among you." Joel 2:25

g) *To break the yoke of hereditary curse* (further to certain acts made by the parents or grandparents)

As already stated before, the chastening for the sins of a person is fully endured by herself, yet the consequences may also impact the next generations after her. Some people feel the impact of the sins of their parents as natural consequences of their disobedience. So, we must understand that God does not hold us guilty of the sins of our parents, but we may endure their consequences.

By confessing their sins and prayer of cancellation, the yoke of the hereditary curse can lose its power.

"In those days they shall say no more: "The fathers have eaten sour grapes, and the children's teeth are set on edge." Jeremiah 31:29

"What do you mean when you use this proverb concerning the land of Israel, saying: The fathers have eaten sour grapes, and the children's teeth are set on edge?" Ezekiel 18:2

h) *To break every satanic regulation and dominion on your progress* (Luke 13:16)

In their work of systematic destruction, the devil and his demons always seek to regulate and dominate over man's progress. They spiritually raise up walls which prevent you from accessing real progress. Thus, through confession and prayer of faith, we can break all his regulations and dominions over our lives.

"So ought not this woman, being a daughter of Abraham, whom Satan has bound – think of it – for eighteen years, be loosed from this bond on the Sabbath?" Luke 13:16

"Behold, I give you the authority to trample on serpents and scorpions, and over all the power of the enemy, and nothing shall by any means hurt you." Luke 10:19

i) **To ask God the power for explosive breakthroughs and to reject little breakthrough in Jesus' name**

General prosperity has always been God's desire for His own. This is why He equips us with natural and supernatural capacities that can lead us to experience explosive breakthrouhgs!

"And when your herds and your flocks multiply, and your silver and your gold are multiplied, and all that you have is multiplied." Deuteronomy 8:13

"And the Lord will grant you plenty of goods, in the fruit of your body, in the increase of your livestock, and in the produce of your ground, in the land of which the Lord swore to your fathers to give you." Deuteronomy 28:11

j) **To break the power of incantations (words and acts) and rituals** against your life and your destiny

Every incantatory word and act raised against your life with the purpose to maintain you in established spiritual laws and in maleficent prison can be cancelled and destroyed by the power of prayer and deliverance which is the name of Jesus Christ.

Chap 3: Parents' sins and maleficent inheritance: how to get out of it?

"In righteousness you shall be established; you shall be far from oppression, for you shall not fear ; and from terror, for it shall not come near you. Indeed they shall surely assemble, but not because of Me. Whoever assembles against you shall fall for your sake. Behold, I have created the blacksmith who blows the coals in the fire, who brings forth an instrument for his work; and I have created the spoiler to destroy. No weapon formed against you shall prosper, and every tongue which rises against you in judgement you shall condemn. This is the heritage of the servants of the Lord, and their righteousness is from Me." Isaiah 54:14-17.

"Behold, I give you the authority to trample on serpents and scorpions, and over all the power of the enemy, and nothing shall by any means hurt you." Luke 10:19

"Death and life are at the power of the tongue, and those who love it will eat its fruit." Proverbs 18:21

TO OVERCOME THE WEIGHT OF THE PAST THAT PURSUES YOU AND THAT CRUCHES YOU

CHAPTER 4

GUILT AND FORGIVENESS TO OTHERS: A KEY STEP OF HEALING OF THE PAST

4.1 GUILT

Some believers are found in the prison of guilt. They feel guilty for the sins they committed in the past, even after their repentance and conversion. Whereas generally, these sins were committed before the person became a child of God. So, in order to settle the matter clearly, we will deal with all kinds of guilt that the devil imposes on men, with regards to sins both before and after conversion. ...

4.1.1. To acknowledge sin as sin

It is hard for a believer to be liberated from the prison of guilt if he does not first acknowledge sin as sin. To acknowledge sin as such means to call the sin by name and that things are clearly shown to the Lord, even though He is omniscient.

4.1.2 The true confession

When the person has called the sin by its name, the Lord can help her to see things the way they are before God. This leads man to admit his sins to the Lord. Proverbs 28:13 says:
"He who covers his sins will not prosper, but whoever confesses and forsakes them will have mercy."

And Psalm 32:5:

"I acknowledged my sin to You, and my iniquity I have not hidden. I said, "I will confess my transgressions to the Lord," and You forgave the iniquity of my sin."

Confession must not be done anyhow, but sincerely. It is useless to confess the sin without radically put an end to it once for all. For when we confess, God does not only hear our words. He will look at our heart to check (if) whether there is hatred for sin, and whether or not the person made the firm decision to leave her sin.

"If we confess our sins, He is faithful and just to forgive us our sins and to cleanse from all unrighteousness." 1 John 1:9

Chap 4: Guilt and forgiveness to others: a key step of healing of the past

"The Lord is merciful and gracious, slow to anger, and abounding in mercy. He will not always strive with us, nor will He keep His anger forever. He has not dealt with us according to our sins, nor punished us according to our iniquities. For as heaven are high above the earth, so great is His mercy toward those who fear Him; as far as the east is from the west, so far has He removed our transgressions from us. As a father pities his children, so the Lord pities those who fear Him. For He knows our frame; He remembers that we are dust." Psalm 103:8-14

4.1.3 Acceptation of God's forgiveness

Many are those who find it hard to accept God's forgiveness and to forgive themselves. The lack of an authentic and true repentance may lead the believer to this stage. The true repentance provokes a change of heart, of behaviour, of thoughts and attitudes. True repentance implies that the person realised the nature of her sin and understood it was a transgression against God. This person is not first worried by the consequence of her sin on herself but is rather worried about what her sin caused to God (to His glory, His holiness, His honour…). She repents first because she caused a dishonour to the Lord. After having taken this step, she can now consider the second consequence of her sin which has an impact on her future, on her present, on her relationship with other people.

False repentance leads to a false confidence and to a false forgiveness, and the proof of the falseness is that you always commit the same sin. Those who repent truly fall rarely into the same sin. Since God accepted the person and forgave her, He also removed the eternal consequences of her sins.

4.1.4 From forgiveness to liberation.

Someone who does not forgive shuts the door to the healing and liberating action of the father and chooses the way that leads to death. He participates to the work of the devil. On the contrary, someone who

forgives is open to the healing and liberating action of the father and chooses the way that leads to life. He participates to His work, letting Him be God.
What forgiveness is :

1) It is neither a bargaining or an exchange; but is rather a favour, which is granted and founded on the gratefulness towards Christ, separating the sinner from his sin.
"Therefore be merciful, just as your Father also is merciful." Luke 6:36.
"Bearing with one another, and forgiving one another, if anyone has a complaint against another; even as Christ forgave you, so you also must do." Colossians 3:13.
"Then he knelt down and cried out with a loud voice, "Lord, do not charge them with this sin." And as he said this, he fell asleep." Acts 7:60.

2) It is not an emotion of the heart, but rather a decision of the will, founded on Christ's will to give up holding anything against the guilty.
"And whenever you stand praying, if you have anything against anyone, forgive him, that your Father in heaven may also forgive you your trespasses." Mark 11:25
"Judge not, and you shall not be judged. Condemn not, and you shall not be condemned. Forgive, and you will be forgiven." Luke 6:37

"And forgive us our debts, as we forgive our debtors." Matthew 6:12

3) It is not the minimization of the fault but rather a settled bill, founded on the atonement of Christ, and releasing the guilty from the deserved sentence.
"For this is My blood of the new covenant, which is shed for many for the remission of sins." Matthew 26:28
"And He Himself is the propitiation for our sins, and not for ours only but also for the whole world." 1John 2:2

4) It is not the making guilty of the person herself, but the release of the guilty one, founded on the example of Christ, accepting personal consequences. In our context, making guilty and guilt are two things distinct. On one hand, guilt refers to admitting being guilty of the fault that was really committed; whereas on the other hand, making guilty refers to the guilt for a fault that we think we committed, or a suggested guilt.
"She said, "No one, Lord." And Jesus said to her, "Neither do I condemn you; go and sin no more." John 8:11
"Then Jesus said, "Father, forgive them, for they do not know what they do." Luke 23:34
"Who Himself bore our sins in His own body on the tree, that we, having died to sins, might live for righteousness - by whose stripes you were healed." 1 Pierre 2:24

5) It is not the distancing from the other person, but an unconditional acceptation, founded on the love of Christ, who was praying, doing good.
"But God demonstrates His own love toward us, in that while we were still sinners, Christ died for us." Romans 5:8
"But I say to you, love your enemies, bless those who curse you, do good to those who hate you, and pray for those who spitefully use you and persecute you." Matthew 5:44

6) It is not an isolated and calculated act, but a wisdom from above and that is founded on Christ's teaching to forgive as long as there is something to forgive.
"But the wisdom that is from above is first pure, then peaceable, gentle, willing to yield, full of mercy and good fruits, without partiality." James 3:17.
"And you, being dead in your trespasses and the circumcision of your flesh, He has made alive together with Him, having forgiven you all trespasses." Colossians 2:13

7) It is not the repression in memory, but the resolution to set it aside, based on God's character, removing the painful memories.
"And be kind to one another, tenderhearted, forgiving one another, even as God in Christ forgave you." Ephesians 4:32
"If we confess our sins, He is faithful and just to forgive us our sins and to cleanse us from all unrighteousness." 1 John 1:9

8) It is not a superficial politeness, but a love commitment, founded on Christ's character, seeking to lift up the guilty.

"Moreover if your brother sins against you, go and tell him his fault between you and him alone. If he hears you, you have gained your brother." Matthew 18:15

"Therefore, as the elect of God, holy and beloved, put on tender mercies, kindness, humility, meekness, longsuffering." Colossians 3:12

So is the process of full restoration in Jesus Christ.

4.1.5 The act of restitution

"Then, Zacchaeus stood and said to the Lord, "Look, Lord, I give half of my goods to the poor; and if I have taken anything from anyone by false accusation, I restore fourfold." And Jesus said to him, "Today, salvation has come to this house, because he also is a son of Abraham." Luke 19:8-9

"If a person sins and commits a trespass against the Lord by lying to his neighbour about what was delivered to him for safekeeping, or about a pledge, or about a robbery, or if he has extorted from his neighbour, or if he has found what was lost and lies concerning it, and swears falsely – in any of these things that a man may do in which he sins; then it shall be, because he has sinned and is guilty, that he shall restore what he has stolen, or the thing which he has extorted, or what was delivered to him for safekeeping, or the lost thing

Chap 4: Guilt and forgiveness to others: a key step of healing of the past

which he found, or all that about which he has sworn falsely. He shall restore its full value, add one -fifth more to it, and give it to whomever it belongs, on the day of the trespass offering. And he shall bring his trespass offering to the Lord, a ram without blemish from the flock, with your valuation, as a trespass offering, to the priest. So the priest shall make atonement for him before the Lord, and he shall be forgiven for any one of these things that he may have done in which he trespasses." Leviticus 6:2-7

"If a thief is found breaking in, and he is struck so that he dies, there shall be no guilt for his bloodshed. If the sun has risen on him, there shall be guilt for his bloodshed. He should make full restitution; if he has nothing, then he shall be sold for his theft. If the theft is certainly found alive in his hand, whether it is an ox or donkey or sheep, he shall restore double. If a man causes a field or vineyard to be grazed, and lets loose his animal, and it feeds in another man's field, he shall make restitution from the best of his own field and from the best of his own vineyard. [...]." Exodus 22:2-9

Some still bear on them the weight of guilt of their past, even after a real repentance and a true restoration from God. This is not due to their relationship with God, but rather to their relationship with man, for the consequences of sin must be solved. The relationship the believer has with people may affect his relationship with God. This is the reason why the act of restitution allows us to sort things out with men after we sorted them out with God in repentance and confession.

For this purpose, the prayer of preparation is important and consists in praying God to touch and prepare the person who is wounded and to grant you His grace to forgive you. You must pray both before proceeding to the act of restitution, and after, for God to heal the wounds you caused. The purpose of this act is to lead the person who was offended to a position similar, as much as possible, to the position she should have if the offense had not occurred. In this process, it is important to let the Holy Spirit guide you for there are deep aspects which imply the Holy Spirit's intervention and assistance. When the restitution is not achieved in accordance with the Holy Spirit's requirements, constant troubles may occur in an area of your life because of your fundamental refusal to step in this process.

CHAPTER 5
THE IMPACT OF CHILDHOOD IN ADULT LIFE

5.1 INTRODUCTION

"Train up a child in the way he should go, and when he is old, he will not depart from it." Proverbs 22:6

This verse is one of the most well-known verses about the education of children, but maybe not the most understood in its spiritual meaning. The Hebrew word for "to teach" is "hanak", which means "to dedicate". It is used for the inauguration of a house (Deuteronomy 20:5), the consecration of the temple (1 Kings 8:63; 2 Chronicles 7:5), and the dedication of an altar (Numbers 7:10; 2 Chronicles 7:9). Here the word "hanak" seems to include the idea of setting apart, restricting, or putting some limits.

To educate children consists in laying some limits to the child's behaviour, in order to turn him away from evil and to guide him in the right direction, the Lord's way.

Gleaser Leonard Archer, an Old Testament theologian, stresses that this Hebrew verb "hanak" is close to the Egyptian "h-n-k" which means "to give to the gods" or "to consecrate for the divine service." He suggests then that the verse 6 may comprise several meanings; to dedicate the child to God, to prepare him for his responsibilities in the future, or to train him for his adult life.

In the way he should go: Many interpretations are found for this expression: either according to the way he should take professionally or morally speaking, or according to the requirements of his personality, of his conduct, or of his age. Since in the Proverbs, the word "way" never means "personality" nor "age", it is prudent to understand it as "a correct way", that is the path of wisdom and righteousness about which so many Proverbs insist. If the child is raised in this righteous way before God, he will not depart from it once he is an adult.

Many people today result from the things that happened to them in their childhood (the past). Many of the things that occur during childhood may have serious consequences on adult life and govern negatively the personality, the character, the perception of an individual.

5.2 SOME PRACTICAL EXAMPLES

In this chapter we will give some practical illustrations that will help us to understand our issue.

- *Permanent criticism and lack of congratulations* for an effort or a success, which may establish in the child's mind this idea that he/she is a failure, a good-for-nothing.

  This may also result in an attitude of superiority, of feeling contempt for others, of desiring to be seen and praised, of always be willing others to say good things about him/her, of striving to dominate over everybody, avoiding all those who look better than him/her, rejecting all suggestions or remarks even the most reasonable and most constructive for his/her life.

- *Ill-treatments and wickedness* shown to the child by the step-mother, step-father, or any other person in the childhood, who may establish a feeling of total rejection in his/her adult life, and cause consequently self-pity, withdrawal and inability to come to terms with himself/herself.

- *The abandonment of the child by his parents*, for any reason, may develop in him the feeling of being totally undesirable, which produces in adult life a rejection for any mark of love and affection that may be expressed to him/her. This eventually settles a feeling of fear and love for loneliness, for the presence of people could then be a threat.

- *The marked preference and rejection of the parents* for one of the children may result in the development of hardness of heart in the other children, due to the lack of love. It may also cause a lack of pity while he always seeks to be accepted, and the inability to give love because he has not received any. Every people around him at an adult age may (his wife, his children, his parents, even some friends…) may feel the impact of the love he was deprived.

- *The loss of a father or mother at an early age* may also cause men to have that strong desire that their wife should be both the wife but also the mum; and in the same way will cause women to desire that their husband be both the husband and the dad.

- *The illegitimacy of the child* may result in deep feeling of insecurity, a growing failure to be a boy or a girl without any father to the other's sight.

- ***Insecure living conditions*** (absolute poverty) which may result in the attachment to useful or useless things, which lead to be prisoner from material goods.

- ***Parent's negative words about the physical aspect of the children*** may result in the development of complexes in their adult life and reduce their efforts by preventing them from using their potential of success.

All these examples clearly show that most people react depending on what happened to them during their childhood. The serious impact of childhood on adult life requires for the children to be treated carefully, and for this purpose, the parents must associate the Lord Jesus Christ in the education of their children.

5.3 GOD'S SOLUTION

Often, men try to solve by themselves the negative impacts and the deep consequences of the childhood on adult life, through psychiatrists or psychologists, which could bring a certain relief. But to get a deep, efficient, and permanent solution to these problems, man must look at his creator who holds the greatest strength and power. Man needs thus to cooperate with God so that God's solutions may be tangible. This is the process to follow:

- **Accept the reality of this impact** which greatly influenced your childhood. You endure some consequences in your personality, character... and you wonder about your origins. You must identify where the problem is. The Holy Spirit's assistance is necessary in this process. If you do not identify the origin of the problem, you must ask Him to reveal it to you. He can remind you what you need to know about your past, for your deliverance and restoration.

- **Give thanks to God for these events** which occurred in your past. We often ask ourselves why we should give thanks to God, but this is very efficient in the life of whoever does it (1 Thessalonians 5:18-19; Ephesians 5:20; Colossians 3:17). Thanksgiving for all things and for all circumstances is an act of submission to the Lord. This is a way to tell God: "Father, you knew that this event was about to take place in my life, and you could prevent it from happening, but you decided not to do it. You allowed it to take place, for this was used to achieve in me something greater and better than the evil already caused in my life." The person who thanks God provokes Him for the second touch or for particular touch. She no more hates this event and is not ashamed anymore, nor of the event nor of the consequences. She accepts herself before being restored.

- **Introduce your problem to God and believe He comes to help you,** for faith plays a great part in the process of deliverance from its consequences. It is important, whenever it is possible, to open your heart and to share with somebody who will support you in this process. This person should be trustable, with spiritual maturity, having a good knowledge of the Word of God and knowing how to minister under the total leadership of the Holy Spirit.

"Call upon Me in the day of trouble; I will deliver you, and you will glorify Me." Psalm 50:15

TO OVERCOME THE WEIGHT OF THE PAST THAT PURSUES YOU AND THAT CRUCHES YOU

CHAPTER 6

THE SIN OF COMPARISON AND ITS CONSEQUENCES

"So David went out wherever Saul sent him, and behaved wisely. And Saul set him over the men of war, and he was accepted in the sight of all the people and also in the sight of Saul's servants. Now it had happened as they were coming home, when David was returning from the slaughter of the Philistine, that the women had come out of all the cities of Israel, singing and dancing, to meet King Saul, with tambourines, with joy, and with musical instruments. So the women sans as they danced, and said: "Saul has slain his thousands, and David his ten thousands." Then Saul was very angry, and the saying displeased him; and he said, "They have ascribed to David ten thousands, and to me they have ascribed only thousands. Now what more can he have *but the kingdom?" So Saul eyed David from that day forward."* 1 Samuel 18:5-9

David was not simply chosen from eternity to become the founder of the royal messianic dynasty but the Lord in his providence, also prepared him to take his responsibilities of king. David had served as a shepherd in the field and had a heart of a loving and protective shepherd, which are qualities that are suitable for a king. He had learned the sense of responsibilities and courage while facing savage beasts which were threatening the flock (1 Samuel 17:34-36). He had learned to play the harp, an art that made him to be sensitive and that would make him to compose touching psalms which exalt the Lord and celebrate his great deeds. David had been brought to the royal palace as a musician and as a fighter, in order to get some experience in the leadership of a state. Even though he had no training at the time of his consecration, he was remarkably well prepared to become king of Israel when he was crowned some fifteen years later. The more his popularity increased, the more his relationship with Saul deteriorated, for the king had become seriously jealous. In fact, his continuous comparison with David pushed him to sin (jealousy, plot, attempt of murder). He realized that David had become the new hero of Israel. The day following the dramatic victory of David over Goliath,

Saul brought him again to the palace, but this time, as the head of his men of war (1 Samuel 18:5). David's privileged position in the court was also reinforced by his friendship with Jonathan, Saul's eldest son. This divine attachment became so strong that Jonathan, although he was supposed to be heir of the throne of Israel, deprived himself of his own royal insignia and gave them to David, acknowledging this way his divine election to the office of king (1 Samuel 18:4; 23:17). The pact of friendship made between David and Jonathan gave one more advantage to David, who became so efficient on the military front that his valiant works were well-known everywhere. Saul became furious at the sight of his own glory being tarnished, and, under a demonic influence, comparison led him to strike David with his spear (1 Samuel 18:10-11; 19:9-10). Nevertheless, God delivered David and made him to become even more popular.

Saul ended up hating the song of 1 Samuel 18 21:11 (1 Samuel 18:5-7) because it gave more honour to David than to him. This comparison produced jealousy. Since then, Saul's jealousy and wickedness towards David were manifest. In some way, he was acknowledging himself that David was the legitimate heir of the throne, which Samuel had talked about in Gilgal (1 Samuel 15:28). Comparison produced three things in him which prevented him from seeing David as God's answer in front of the enemies of Israel:

1. He was raging (state of anger for things which we did not care about before)

2. He could not stand the situation (due to a wrong perception)

3. He looked at David with spite, which resulted into hatred, animosity, lack of indulgence.

David was prospering everywhere Saul sent him, which shows the level of submission that David had for Saul. If we do not submit to our spiritual leaders, to the authority under which we are established, nobody will submit to our own authority once we will be elevated at our turn.

David had never been to war. Yet God had equipped and qualified him for that. He became the head of the men of war. God's favour was upon him, and this allowed him to also get the favour of men. The Bible states that he pleased the whole people, even the servants of Saul.

6.1 DEFINITION AND CONSEQUENCES OF COMPARISON

Comparison may be defined as the action of comparing people or things, to examine their similarities and their differences. It is also to confront two different realities with a tool of comparison (such as, like, looking like, similar to, more than, less than etc.).

One of the characteristics that are manifested in the life of people who are not healed from their negative past is the sin of comparison. This sin leads to a life of bitterness, frustration etc. And this sin has a main root which is covetousness, usually expressed in several areas of life: social, intellectual, physical, affective, material, professional, financial, etc. The sin of covetousness results in many behaviours. Those who are affected by it always compare what they have with what the others have and are never satisfied. This cause them to sink into a restless life. Actually, this sin arouses in you unsatisfied desires and ends up causing serious damage to the soul and in life. Covetousness leads to jealousy, strife, and division.

6.2 SOLUTIONS

One of the main source of covetousness is self-rejection. It is then very important to accept yourself and to realize that you are a unique individual. You do not need what belongs to someone else to feel better. Realize that you are the best person to achieve what you are called to do. God's plan for your life is far better than any other plan you or anyone else in the whole creation could imagine for you. Accept God's will.

"And do not be conformed to this world, but be transformed by the renewing of your mind, that you may prove what is that good and acceptable and perfect will of God." Romans 12:2

To conform is to adopt an external expression which does not reflect what is truly inside, a kind of masquerade. The word implies that the readers of Paul's letter were living like this. He exhorted them to stop behaving this way. All contemporary thoughts and values fashion the moral atmosphere of our world and are always dominated by Satan (2 Corinthians 4:4). As well as Christ revealed outwardly and shortly his divine inward nature and his glory during the Transfiguration, so the christians should manifest their inward redeemed nature, not only once, but every single day (2 Corinthians 3:18; Ephesians 5:18). Once renewed, the believer is soaked with the Word of God and controlled by it. The Holy Spirit transforms his thought through the regular study and meditation of the Holy Scriptures, which becomes his main reference. So many people feel they are less good, less efficient, less beautiful, less thin, less intelligent, less interesting etc. But it is possible to get rid of our complexes.

Chap 6: The sin of comparison and its consequences

- **To regain self-confidence by relying on what God says that we are.**

Please do this useful exercise: Try to look back in time and, in a neutral way, observe the way you perceive yourself. Evaluate as well the way you respond to other people's comments. This will help you to check whether you give more consideration to what people around you think about you or expect from you.

"I said, "You are gods, and all of you are children of the Most High. But you shall die like men, and fall like one of the princes." Psalm 82:6-7

"Here am I and the children whom the Lord has given me! We are for signs and wonders in Israel from the Lord of hosts, who dwells in Mount Zion." Isaiah 8:18

"You are of God, little children, and have overcome them, because He who is in you is greater than he who is in the world." 1 John 4:4

"You are the light of the world. A city that is set on a hill cannot be hidden. Nor do they light a lamp and put it under a basket, but on a lampstand, and it gives light to all who are in the house." Matthew 5:14-15

Your greatness is in God. You can do all things by He who strengthens you.

- *To acknowledge our defects and to see our qualities.*

Sometimes, our complexes come from our inability to see our strengths. We obviously tend to zoom on our defects and minimize all our qualities. In this case, here is what I suggest you: list all your strengths (physical, psychological, and spiritual) in order that you see your life more positively. Rely on the grace of God which perfects you.

2 Corinthians 12:9-10:

"And He said to me, "My grace is sufficient for you, for My strength is made perfect in weakness." Therefore most gladly I will rather boast in my infirmities, that the power of Christ may rest upon me. Therefore I take pleasure in infirmities, in reproaches, in needs, in persecutions, in distresses, for Christ's sake. For when I am weak, then I am strong."

God's grace is constantly available, the weaker the human instrument is, the more the grace of God is shown. Paul was not pleased in the pain itself, but he rejoiced that the power of Christ could thus be revealed even more through him.

- *Value your difference*

Not to be like everybody is not a defect. It is even a quality. Do not be bothered then to be who you are and take your place. Obviously this is not automatic, but day by day, make a step to accept you better.

- *Do not keep everything for you*

Find somebody fearing and loving God with whom you can talk freely about what you feel. She will be able to help you to discern the good and bad impressions which you have about yourself. You can also keep a personal diary to get rid of your worries and burdens. While reading it, you will be able to take a distance and to balance the whole thing.

- *Get rid of evil relationships*

Sometimes we have a tendency to surround ourselves with toxic people: they judge us severely, criticize us, cause us to doubt, and give us evil counsels. To be surrounded by negative people will slow down our zeal for success and victory in Jesus Christ. Maybe it is time for you to check your relationships or to clarify some things with them.

- *To be able to acknowledge and use what the other people have received from God.*

Contrary to Saul, Jonathan his son, who was supposed to inherit the throne of Israel, has shown a different attitude. He took off his own royal insignias and gave them to David. He was able to take advantage of the pact of friendship concluded with David. He did not look at David as an enemy or as a competitor, but rather recognized in him the Lord's answer for Israel and acknowledged his divine election to the office of king. Many people miss God's graces and blessings because of a wrong perception of things and men, due to jealousy, pride, and fear to see someone else to be appreciated. To learn to recognize what God has placed in other people will set you in a position of grace and will open you doors to benefit fully from this grace and to be connected to it.

Man is and remains the main means of God to fulfil His plans on the earth. Learn to appreciate and to acknowledge what other people have received from God, bearing in mind that God is a God of abundance, and that He will bless us at the appointed time. Do not fall into the trap of complexes of inferiority, of jealousy, of rejection, which may make you slaves of the sin of comparison, and prevent you from seeing God's answer through others. For the Bible declares, *"Who has first given to Him and it shall be repaid to him?" For of Him and through Him and to Him are all things, to whom be glory forever." Romans 11:35-36*

- *Do not live in false illusions*

When you struggle with multiple complexes, you often confuse everything. You believe that you missed your promotion because of your 10kg overweight. Stop repeating over and over everything you are not (evil, uninteresting, stupid, ugly, etc...)

To conclude, the trap of comparison is the fear to be compared. You are the only one to be you. Learn not to judge your knowledge, your experience, your skills compared to the others'. The level of comparison is the level of quality of an adjective expressed with regards to a certain reference. Your only true reference in your life must be the will and the Word of God, for you are what God says that you are.

The Bible says in Psalm 91:2-3:

"I will say of the Lord, "He is my refuge and my fortress; my God, in Him I will trust." Surely, He shall deliver you from the snare of the fowler and from the perilous pestilence."

In the middle of spiritual warfare which we may face, the awareness of the presence of God and of His love for us is not sufficient to remain victorious. Being overcomer in Jesus Christ, you need to believe what the Word of God says about you, and to know also how to declare it continuously. Proclaim it to the ears of the devil and of his agents. Declare it when things go well for you, and even when the enemy tries to trouble you. Continue to declare with conviction what the God's Word says about your life in terms of health, business, marriage, plans, ministry... in your walk with Him. Do not keep quiet, for your silence is responsible for the blows you often receive from the enemy. Do not allow the devil to maintain you in bondage trying to make you believe that the Gospel is powerless. Do not be deceived while neglecting the importance of declaring what God says about you.

I declare in Jesus' name that you are victorious in this situation you face. Receive the spiritual strength from the Holy Spirit. Declare what God says about you in His Word and fight boldly by faith refusing to be intimidated by the devil and the demons.

N.B. What you cannot declare, you cannot possess it neither.

CHAPTER 7

REJECTION AND ITS CONSEQUENCES IN ADULT LIFE

"Then the Lord turned to him and said," Go in this might of yours, and you shall save Israel from the hand of the Midianites. Have I not sent you?" So he said to Him," O my Lord, how can I save Israel? Indeed my clan is the weakest in Manasseh, and I am the least in my father's house." And the Lord said to him," Surely I will be with you, and you shall defeat the Midianites as one man." Judges 6:14-16

This text relates the calling of Gideon by the Angel of the Lord. We must precise that Gideon's story does not start by a statement like "God gave a deliverer named Gideon!", but rather by a description of the method used by God to raise him. This teaches us several things:

- First of all, God does not call qualified men but men who are willing to, and He qualifies them for the task there are called to do.

- Secondly, He uses things that are despised to shame the wise.

- Thirdly, He can take somebody very low and elevate him very high.

- Fourthly, He does with the man who is willing to things that do not correspond to where he comes from... There are many lessons to learn here from this passage but let us focus on our topic.

Here, Gideon's mission comes after a confrontation with the angel of the Lord (who is the Lord), who appeared in front of him as a stranger passing by and who sat under the terebinth tree in Ophrah. Joash, Gideon's father, was from Abiezer's family, one of Manasseh's clans (Joshua 17:2). Ophrah could not be mistaken for the site from Benjamin's territory, but had to be located around the border of Manasseh, in the valley of Jizreel. Nowadays, potential sites were identified such as El-Affula (10km on the east of Meguiddo) or Et-Taiyibi (Hapharaïm, 8km from Beth-Shan).

The fact that Gideon was threshing wheat in the winepress reveals both his fear to be seen by the

Midianites ́ and the poverty of the harvest. For normally, wheat was threshed (seed separated from the stalk) in an area of wheat, in open air (1 Chronicles 21:20-23), by oxen drawing a cart.

The angel starts by declaring that the Lord is with Gideon and describes him as a mighty man of valor, in other words, "strong and mighty man". Here, even this description of Gideon is somewhat satirical. The angel of the Lord makes it on purpose, in order to announce a change. Gideon could perceive it as a mockery, for at that time, he was far from being a valiant hero. The angel of the Lord probably revealed him, on one hand, the potential he would have once the Spirit would come upon him, and on the other hand, his rank of noble man in the community. God knows your future and the plans of happiness He prepares you. No matter how painful your past was, you can trust Him for a better future. Do not allow doubt or lack of confidence to become obstacles to God's plans in your life. Gideon was questioning God's divine promise because of the conditions which his people was living in at that time. And he concludes with exactitude that the Lord had delivered them into the hands of the Midianites.

The angel of the Lord spoke again as a divine person, saying to Gideon: *"Go and save Israel from*

Madian's hand." The expression "in this might of yours" confirms the assurance of the divine presence mentioned before (v12). Gideon objected saying, *"My family is the weakest [...] and I am the least."* His objection, although it reflected the Near Eastern culture typical modesty, was also an observation. God is willing to work with man in the achievement of His plans based on his faith in His might, for faith is not unaware of the reality nor limited by it, but is rather based on the divine Word (the truth). Finally, God ensured Gideon of His presence *"I will be with you"*. Be aware of the presence of God with you, which allows you to overcome rejection and its consequences.

"Gideon said to the Lord, "If You will save Israel by my hand as You have said – look, I shall put a fleece of wool on the threshing floor; if there is dew on the fleece only, and it is dry on all the ground, then I shall know that You will save Israel by my hand., as You have said." And it was so. When he rose early the next morning and squeezed the fleece together, he wrung the dew out of the fleece, a bowlful of water. Then Gideon said to God,"Do not be angry with me, but let me speak just once more; let me test, I pray, just once more with the fleece; let it now be dry only on the fleece, but on all the ground let there be dew." Judges 6:36-40

Asking for a miracle from God as a sign (Matthew 12:38; 1 Corinthians 1:22-23), Gideon is showing a surprising lack of faith for a man whose name is written ~~on~~ among the top heroes of faith (Hebrew 11:32)! And it is even more surprising that he already had received a sign from God at the time of his calling (Judges 6:17-21). This new sign consisted rather in a confirmation or an assurance of God's presence or divine power for the task to achieve. God still responded to him, despite the weakness of his faith and saturated the fleece of wool with dew. There was so much dew that Gideon could fill a full bowl with it. This leads us to understand that God's blessing does not depend on the people who surround us nor the context in which we live but on our obedience towards God. Gideon may have had this in mind, for it could be that the ground gets naturally dry before the fleece.

This reflects also an attitude of insensitivity and unbelief that is sometimes manifested when God makes wonders in our lives, and we see them like deserved rewards, which prevents us from abounding in thanksgiving. This is the reason why he asked for a second sign, opposite to the previous one: *"Let it now be dry only on the fleece, but on all the ground let there be dew."* God patiently answered to his desire, in order to teach him that in spite of an environment favourable to success and victory, every true success result from the obedience to His Word. It explains the failures of all those who want to operate in disobedience. This reassured Gideon regarding the fulfilment of his mission.

7.1 TO BECOME A FULFILLED ADULT AFTER HAVING BEEN A REJECTED CHILD

(Gideon, Joseph)

7.1.1. Expression and consequences of rejection

The fear of rejection is developed during childhood and it has multiple causes (Parents' criticism, neglect or absence, undesired pregnancy etc.).

The damages may be devastating for the child who, at an adult age, will set himself in conditions of rejection facing his employers, his friends, his family etc. This adult will often be neurotic, out of touch with reality, unable to be consistent or to talk sense, and will become unhappy.

What hurts more is not so much to be rejected by the others, but it is rather the way this rejection is interpreted which is the real problem.

Joseph, David, the prophets of the Old Testament, and even Christ, have all been rejected by their brothers. Yet they did not make it a major problem which would have pushed them to depression or any other psychotic state. At an adult age, many people live with a feeling of rejection which condemns them to lack self-confidence. This paralyzes them and prevents them from daring anything and ends up with strangling their potential. Gideon responded this way when answered to God that he was not able to save the people because he was part of the poorest family. But God did not listen to his lack of self-confidence and helped him to go beyond his doubts, saying:

"Then the Lord turned to him and said, "Go in this might of yours, and you shall save Israel from the hand of the Midianites." Judges 6:14

If Gideon had been paralyzed by his feeling of inability, he would not have done anything. But God helped him to go beyond his doubts and this allowed him to deliver Israel.

The children who felt rejected will suffer from a feeling of abandonment which is among the greatest affective wounds. Here are some examples of behaviours generally observed in their lives:

- They **will often abandon their partners** rather than they will be abandoned.

- They will suffer from **chronic serious anguish** and from stress.

- They will end up being **aggressive and likely to live on the fringe of the society.**

- They will find it **hard to accept themselves,** will doubt about their value.

- They will often be **dependent in the affective area,** with a possibility to remain alone.

- They will need to see very often some **proofs of affection** from their partners (which will end up discouraging the partners).

- They will leave with the **fear to be abandoned,** rejected, left alone.

Decision to make: what is done is over; it is past! Give thanks to God. It is important to make the decision to get out of it, for God only intervenes if we are willing to change. Do not stay in a position of victim going nowhere.

7.1.2 God's solutions for restoration from rejection

- *God has great plans for you. Do not allow the failures of the past to paralyze you.* If you are held in rejection, you prevent the potential God placed in you to be expressed. Break its power and dominion in the name of Jesus Christ. This is one of the most important steps to develop and achieve God's great plans for your life.

"For I know the thoughts that I think toward you, says the Lord, thoughts of peace and not of evil, to give you a future and a hope." Jeremiah 29:11

- **No matter what are your trials and failures you experienced in the past, it does not reduce your value.** Even wounded by life, God loves you. Break this feeling of rejection and accept yourself as you are, for you are a wonderful creature (Psalm 139:14):

"I will praise You, for I am fearfully and wonderfully made. Marvelous are Your works, all that my soul knows very well."

"Be silent, all flesh, before the Lord, for He is aroused from His holy habitation!" Zechariah 2:13

"My mouth shall speak the praise of the Lord, and all flesh shall bless His holy name forever and ever." Psalm 145:21

-**The reconciliation with God and with your inner child** who was hurt, ill-treated, and who needs to be cared for (by the Holy Spirit).

"For if when we were enemies we were reconciled to God through the death of His Son, how much more, having been reconciled, we shall be saved by His life." Romans 5:10

"And you, who once were alienated and enemies in your mind by wicked works, yet now He has reconciled in the *body of His flesh through death to present you holy, and blameless, and above reproach in His sight."* Colossians 1:21-22

-*Work on the value and the reliability of what God says about who you are.* You must bear in mind that it was not because you were wicked, or uninteresting, or stupid, or disappointing, which justifies your parents' behaviour, but rather the fact that they were not ready to play their role for some reason, or because their own parents did not give them appropriate counsel to become good parents.

"For I am the Lord, Your God, the Holy One of Israel, Your Saviour; I gave Egypt for your ransom, Ethiopia and Seba in your place. Since you were precious in My sight, you have been honoured, and I have loved you: therefore I will give men for you, and people for your life." Isaiah 43:3-4

7.2 YOU WERE NOT REJECTED BUT NOT WELL-LOVED

You wished you had a mother or a father more like this or less like that in order to feel fine but we encourage you to forget about this ideal parent whom you would have liked to have. For they might not change, but you, you can change the perception you have of your childhood, and leave your painful past behind, because this prevents you to move forward.

7.2.1 Solutions
- *Change perspective*

"Deliver me, O my God, out of the hand of the wicked, out of the hand of the unrighteous and cruel man. For You are my hope, O Lord God; You are my trust from my Youth. By You I have been upheld from birth; You are He who took me out of my mother's womb. My praise shall be continually of You. I have become as a wonder to many, but You are my strong refuge." Psalm 721:4-7

See what this situation could to teach you, and what positive things God extracted from it, since all things work together for good to those who love God and who are the called according to His purpose. Acknowledge the resources which you developed due to this situation (for example: spiritual sensitivity, pleasure of learning, effort to do different things, always moving forward, defence of the most disadvantaged people or of the unloved ones etc.) Troubles that occur in our lives help us to grow, cause us to think about the purpose of life, and send the self to the cross, where it must be crucified. We always face the choice to either learn the lesson from our tough experiences or to remain in the obscurity, contemplating our unhappy past.

-Do not give too much heed to the others opinion and do not evaluate yourself depending on the others' judgement about you. This training involves a good knowledge about yourself. To learn to recognize your weaknesses and strengths and then submit them to the Lord who knows you best and who can help you efficiently and permanently.

"So he went in to Hagar, and she conceived. And when she saw that she had conceived, her mistress became despised in her eyes. Then Saraï said to Abram, "My wrong be upon you! I gave my maid into your embrace; and when she saw that she had conceived, I became despised in her eyes. The Lord judge between me and you and me." Genesis 16:4-5

Saraï was humanly barren, so no heir of the promise could be born of her. This fact pushed Abram and Saraï to commit all kinds of doubtful acts, but Abram learned that God's promise would not be fulfilled this way. According to the customs and law at that time, a barren wife could give her servant to her husband for wife, and the child born from this union was considered as the first wife's child. If the husband said to the son of the slave "You are my son", he became his adoptive son and heir. From this point of view, Saraï's suggestion contained nothing reprehensible. However, with regards to the so clear promise God had made to them, this could only be considered as a questionable act. Then, Saraï's plan, formerly approved by Abram, went all wrong when the Egyptian servant, Hagar, became pregnant, for then, this latter started to despise Saraï. The two women could have wondered about what would happen to Abram's seed. Would it belong to Hagar? Or to Saraï? She left the way of faith, which implies the patient expectation of the fulfilment of God's plan. While choosing this one further to human calculations, Saraï got caught in a series of successive events which pursued her for years. In fact, Ishmael became the ancestors of the Arabs, whose hostility towards the Jews is still at work. Hagar's despise caused Saraï to respond wickedly (Genesis 16:6). She treated Hagar so badly that the latter went away.

We must understand that using human means or solutions which are not inspired by faith, in order to obtain the fulfilment of divine promises, may make the situation to become even more complex, which would be, for sure, an embarrassment. The opinion and the scornful looks which the others may have on us must not prevent us from living happy nor from experiencing the wonderful plan God has for us (Genesis 24:21; 1 Samuel 17:42).

-To be actively involved in sharing with other people

"For as we have many members in one body, but all the members do not have the same function, so we, being many,

are one body in Christ, and individually members of one another." Romans 12:4-5

"Therefore let us not judge one another anymore, but rather resolve this not to put a stumbling block or a cause to fall in our brother's way." Romans 14:13

"Therefore comfort each other and edify one another, just as you also are doing." 1 Thessalonians 5:11

"And let us consider one another in order to stir up love and good works." Hebrews 10:24

-To learn to exist independently of the others' looks.

David, though he was despised, did not care about the evil intentions which his brothers claimed he had, and they could not discourage him with those words. His determination to take up Goliath's challenge did not change since he could not bear the name of the Lord to be insulted again (1 Samuel 17:26-37).

"Now Eliab his oldest brother heard when he spoke to the men; and Eliab's anger was aroused against David, and he said, "Why did you come down here? And with whom have you left those few sheep in the wilderness? I know your pride and the insolence of your heart, for you have come down to see the battle. [...] v30 Then he turned from him toward another [...] v37 Moreover David said, "The Lord, who

delivered me from the paw of the lion and from the paw of the bear, He will deliver me from the hand of this Philistine."

In the New Testament, we can also see the example of John also named Mark: Though he was rejected for a while by Paul (Acts 15:37-40), the Bible shows that he certainly continued to serve God and to do it properly, since Paul could say about him later that he was useful to him for ministry (2 Timothy 4:11).

To be rejected in ministry by somebody such as Apostle Paul was certainly a tough experience for someone who was willing to serve the Lord, taking into account the widespread renown of his ministry, as well as the admiration and fear which the depth of his teachings could cause, but also his blameless attitude, his courage, his perseverance, his endurance in spite of multiple trials (and not the least) which he had gone through, and of which Mark was an eye-witness.

-To speak honestly and to hear carefully, in order to avoid any misunderstandings and a return into the vicious cycle of self-pity and rejection.

"He who speaks truth declares righteousness, but a false witness, deceit. There is one who speaks like the piercings of a sword, but the tongue of the wise promotes health. The truthful lip shall be established forever, but a lying tongue is

but for a moment. Deceit is in the heart of those who devise evil, but counsellors of peace have joy." Proverbs 12:17-20

-*To get out of passiveness,* for to be in a relationship requires some self-investment and work.

"*Give no sleep to your eyes, nor slumber to your eyelids. Deliver yourself like a gazelle from the hand of the hunter, and like a bird from the hand of the fowler.*" Proverbs 6:4-5

"*He who tills his land will be satisfied with bread, but he who follows frivolity is devoid of understanding.*" Proverbs 12:11

"*The lazy man does not roast what he took in hunting, but diligence is man's precious possession.*" Proverbs 12:27

Do not be like those who expect things to happen to them, for success has never occurred by chance but is results rather from planning.

CHAPTER 8

GOD'S PROVISION TO PROBLEMS DUE TO THE IMPACT OF CHILDHOOD ON ADULT LIFE

8.1 MYSTERIES OF DIVINE PROVISION

« *So it was that quails came up at evening and covered the camp, and in the morning the dew lay all around the camp. And when the layer of dew lifted, there, on the surface of the wilderness, was a small round substance, as fine as frost on the ground. So then the children of Israel saw it, they said to one another, What is it?", for they did not know what it was. And Moses said to them, "This is the bread which the Lord has given you to eat. This is the thing which the Lord has commanded: Let every man gather it according to each one's need, one omer for each person, according to the number of persons; let every man tale for those who are in his tent." Then the children of Israel did so and gathered, some more, some less. So when they measured it by omers, he who gathered much had nothing left over, and he who gathered little had no lack. Every man had gathered according to each one's need. And Moses said, "Let no one leave any of it till morning." Notwithstanding they did not heed Moses. But some of them left part of it until morning, and it bred worms and stank. And Moses was angry with them. So they gathered it every morning, every man according to his need. And when became hot, it melted. And so it was, on the sixth day, that they gathered twice as much bread, two omers for each one. And all the rulers of the congregation came and told Moses. Then he said to them"This is what the Lord has said: "Tomorrow is Sabbath rest, a holy Sabbath to the Lord. Bake what you will bake today, and boil what you will boil; and lay up for yourselves all that remains, to be kept until morning." So they laid it up till morning, as Moses commanded; and it did not stink, nor were here any worms in it. Then Moses said, "Eat that today, for today is a Sabbath to the Lord; today you will not find it in the field. Six days you shall gather it, but on the seventh day, the Sabbath, there will be none." Now it happened that some of the people went out on the seventh day to gather, but they found none. And the Lord said to Moses, "How long do you refuse to keep My commandments and My laws? See! For the Lord has given you the Sabbath; therefore He gives you on the sixth day bread for two days. Let every man remain in his place; let no man go out of his place on the seventh day." So the people rested on the seventh day. And the house of Israel called its name Manna. And it was like white coriander seed, and the taste of it was like wafers made with honey. Then Moses said, "This is the thing which the Lord has commanded: "Fill an omer with it, to be kept for your generations, that they may see the bread with which I fed you in the wilderness, when I brought you out of the land of Egypt." And Moses said to Aaron, "Take a pot and put an omer of manna in it, and lay it up before the Lord, to be kept for your generations." Exodus 16:13-35*

Every day, people were gathering the quantity needed only for the day, which implied that the Israelites should trust the Lord for the provision of their food every morning. The sixth day, they had to gather enough for the day as well as for the next day, for there was no bread on the seventh day. Moses and Aaron rebuked the people of Israel for complaining against them and especially against the Lord and reminded them newly about the promise to provide for every need, so that the assembly would know that He is the Lord their God. The Lord continued to provide manna until the nation came to the border of Canaan, where they started to eat the fruits of the land (Joshua 5:12). The manna in the ark was a permanent remembrance of God's faithfulness in providing for all the needs of his people. God shew thus that He could feed and sustain His own.

In the midst of the desert, Israel experienced God's providence:

1. He sent quails (birds)

2. He fed them with bread from heaven (manna)

3. He opened a rock from where water ran out

4. He watered dry places for his people

See how God's miraculous and supernatural provision was a great and tremendous experience for the children of Israel. You can also experience God's provision in your situation, no matter what it is. The supply of manna in the wilderness to the people of Israel such as related in Exodus 16:13-35 illustrates important principles which you must know regarding divine provision.

8.2 GOD'S PRINCIPLES RELATED TO PROVISION

8.2.1 Provision is bound to God's presence in your life

"And in the morning the dew lay all around the camp. And when the layer of dew lifted, there, on the surface of the wilderness, was a small round substance, as fine as frost on the ground. So then the children of Israel saw it, they said to one another, What is it?", for they did not know what it was. And Moses said to them, "This is the bread which the Lord has given you to eat." Exodus 16:13-15

Chap 8: God's provision to problems due to the impact of childhood on adult life

1.   Manna came after the dew, and not before.

2.   The dew symbolizes the manifestation of the presence of God.

3.   The dew symbolizes the presence of the Holy Spirit who is at work in us.

4.   Let us not run first towards provision but let us seek first the presence of God in our lives.

8.2.2 God is the one who sovereignly determines the dimension of the provision you receive

"This is the thing which the Lord has commanded: Let every man gather it according to each one's need, one omer for each person, according to the number of persons; let every man tale for those who are in his tent." Then the children of Israel did so and gathered, some more, some less. So when they measured it by omers, he who gathered much had nothing left over, and he who gathered little had no lack. Every man had gathered according to each one's need." Exodus 16:17-18

1.   God's provision is in proportion with your needs and responsibilities you have.

2.   The greater the mission God called you is and the greater the provision will be.

3.   It is your "right" to ask for more provision in various aspects such as spiritual, material, human, in accordance with your responsibilities.

8.2.3 God's grace, source of your provision

"Six days you shall gather it, but on the seventh day, the Sabbath, there will be none." Now it happened that some of the people went out on the seventh day to gather, but they found none." Exodus 16:26-27

1. Manna was available during six days but not on the seventh day.

2. The simple fact of going out is not enough to find manna, people had to go out the very day God poured it out. This emphasizes the need to learn to walk in the move of the Spirit.

3. This deals with God's grace.

"v26 Look at the birds of the air, for they neither sow nor reap nor gather into barns; yet your heavenly Father feeds them. Are you not of more value than they?" Matthew 6:25-30

"If you then, being evil, know how to give good gifts to your children, how much more will your Father in heaven give good things to those who ask Him!" Matthew 7:11

4. For everything we may have or receive or become, we must be aware of the hand and of the grace of God that are at work behind all this.

"As for every man to whom God has given riches and wealth, and given him power to eat of it, to receive his heritage and rejoice in his labour – this is the gift of God." Ecclesiastes 5:19

5. You will not succeed just because you strove a lot, but because God blessed your efforts.

"And He called his name Noah, saying, "This one will comfort us concerning our work and the toil of our hands because of the ground which the Lord has cursed." Genesis 5:29

"Beware that you do not forget the Lord your God by not keeping His commandments, His judgments, and His statutes as I command you today, lest – when you have eaten and are full, and have built beautiful houses and dwell in them; and when your herds and your flocks multiply, and your silver and gold are multiplied, and all that you have is multiplied, when your heart is lifted, and you forget the Lord your God, who brought you out of the land of Egypt, from the house of bondage." Deuteronomy 8:11-14

6. This is God's grace which arranges for you the times and circumstances.

"And of Joseph he said: "Blessed of the Lord is the land, with the precious things of heaven, with the dew, and the deep lying beneath, with the precious fruits of the sun, with the

precious produce of the months, with the best things of the ancient mountains, with the precious things of the everlasting hills, with the precious things of the earth and its fullness, and the favour of Him who dwells in the bush. Let the blessing come on the head of Joseph, and on the crown of the head of Him who was separate from his brothers." Deuteronomy 33:13-16

7. You must admit, like Paul, that it is by the grace of God that you are who you are.

"But by the grace of God, I am what I am, and His grace towards me was not in vain; but I laboured more abundantly than they all, yet not I, but the grace of God which was with me." 1 Corinthians 15:10

"As for every man to whom God has given riches and wealth, and given him power to eat of it, to receive his heritage and rejoice in his labour – this is the gift of God." Ecclesiastes 5:19

8.2.4 Trust the Provider rather than the provision
"And Moses said, "Let no one leave any of it till morning." Notwithstanding they did not heed Moses. But some of them left part of it until morning, and it bred worms and stank. And Moses was angry with them." Exodus 16:19-20

1. The children of Israel had not to keep some manna for the next morning, except manna of the sixth day.

2. God wants you to learn to lean on Him, on His might, and on His capacity to provide, rather than on your own stock.

3. God is not against savings, but against savings and stocks kept without God.

4. Save up some money, but trust God and He will give you other sources of blessings when your reserves will finish.

8.2.5 God is mighty and able to provide for your needs

"And the house of Israel called its name Manna. And it was like white coriander seed, and the taste of it was like wafers made with honey." Exodus 16:31

1. Coriander was a Mediterranean plant growing in Israel and in Egypt.

2. God gave to his people a Mediterranean plant right in the midst of the wilderness.

3. God can provide beyond what you may think about, beyond what you may expect, above your ways and human considerations.

4. God can surprise you beyond your expectations. Anne asked for one child, but He gave her six. Solomon asked for wisdom, and God gave him on top of it riches, glory, and so many other blessings.

TO OVERCOME THE WEIGHT OF THE PAST THAT PURSUES YOU AND THAT CRUCHES YOU

"Now to Him who is able to do exceedingly abundantly above all what we ask or think, according to the power that works in us." Ephesians 3:20

CHAPTER 9
TO TAKE SPIRITUALLY POSITION

"Then your light shall break forth like the morning, your healing shall spring forth speedily, and your righteousness shall go before you; the glory of the Lord shall be at your rear guard. [...] The Lord will guide you continually, and satisfy your soul in drought, and strengthen your bones; you shall be like a watered garden, and like a spring of water, whose waters do not fail." Isaiah 58:8-11

"Finding out what is acceptable to the Lord. And have no fellowship with the unfruitful works of darkness, but rather expose them." Ephesians 5:10-11

Enter fully into God's plan accepting what He gives you now with the solution of His death and resurrection of His Son Jesus Christ, raised from the dead and sat at the right hand of the Father, interceding for you.

CONFESS THIS WITH ME:

In the name of Jesus Christ, I confess that in Christ I am a new creature. I refuse to be a prisoner of my past and its negative consequences. By the power of the name and of the blood of Jesus, I declare that I am free from all the weight of my disappointments in the past, from all consequences of my parents' sins and maleficent inheritance, from guilt and lack of forgiveness. I accept to forgive and to receive forgiveness. I am liberated from any negative impact of my childhood in my adult life, from rejection, and from the sin of comparison. I seize the whole provision of God for my present life and for my future in the name of Jesus Christ. Amen.

CONTACT THE AUTHOR

Apostle Eddy KADIEBU KANDOLO
Centre Chrétien Bérée
5, Allée Louis de Daubenton
87280 Limoges

www.centrechretienberee.com
Mail: infos@centrechretienberee.com

www.facebook.com/apotreeddykadiebu
www.facebook.com/centrechretienberee

TO OVERCOME THE WEIGHT OF THE PAST THAT PURSUES YOU AND THAT CRUCHES YOU

TO OVERCOME THE WEIGHT OF THE PAST THAT PURSUES YOU AND THAT CRUCHES YOU